PRAISE FOR PREVIOUS EDITIONS OF

South Carolina
Off the Beaten Path ®

"[A] guidebook that captures a South Carolina the
outside world doesn't know about."
—*Carolinian*

"A fun look at our state . . .
a journey with plenty of fascinating byways."
—*State* (Columbia, S.C.)

"Families looking for unusual day trips from Charlotte
will appreciate this guide—complete with user-friendly maps,
fact blocks, and amusing sidebars."
—*Charlotte* (N.C.) *Parent*

Help Us Keep This Guide Up to Date

Every effort has been made by the authors and editors to make this guide as accurate and useful as possible. However, many changes can occur after a guide is published—establishments close, phone numbers change, facilities come under new management, etc.

We would love to hear from you concerning your experiences with this guide and how you feel it could be improved and be kept up to date. While we may not be able to respond to all comments and suggestions, we'll take them to heart, and we'll make certain to share them with the authors. Please send your comments and suggestions to the following address:

The Globe Pequot Press
Reader Response/Editorial Department
P.O. Box 480
Guilford, CT 06437

Or you may e-mail us at: editorial@GlobePequot.com.

Thanks for your input, and happy travels!

OFF THE BEATEN PATH® SERIES

SEVENTH EDITION

OFF THE BEATEN PATH®
SOUTH CAROLINA ➡

A GUIDE TO UNIQUE PLACES

WILLIAM PRICE FOX

**Updated and revised by
J. Michael McLaughlin**

gpp®
travel

Guilford, Connecticut

The prices, rates, and hours listed in this guidebook were con-
firmed at press time. We recommend, however, that you call
establishments to obtain current information before traveling.

To buy books in quantity for corporate use
or incentives, call **(800) 962-0973**
or e-mail **premiums@GlobePequot.com**.

Text design by Linda R. Loiewski
Maps by Equator Graphics © Morris Book Publishing, LLC
Illustrations by Carole Drong
Spot photography throughout © Shutterstock

ISSN 1545-5130
ISBN 978-0-7627-4878-5

Printed in the United States of America

10 9 8 7 6 5 4 3 2 1

Contents

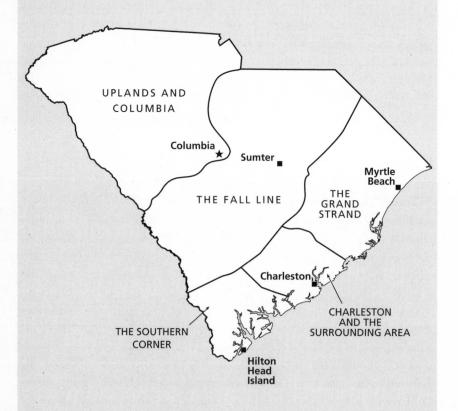

UPLANDS AND
COLUMBIA

Columbia ★

Sumter ■

Myrtle
Beach ■

THE FALL LINE

THE
GRAND
STRAND

Charleston ■

CHARLESTON
AND THE
SURROUNDING AREA

THE SOUTHERN
CORNER

Hilton
Head
Island ■

Introduction

My dad, who spent some time in Europe during World War II and who could hold the center of the room with the best of them, had his own theory about why South Carolina is so different from the rest of the country. When he was in Palermo, he said, he saw a painting of St. George slaying the dragon in which George was more than 6 feet tall and built like a wide receiver. The dragon came in at around 80 hands high, weighing more than fifty tons and throwing out a 60-foot sheet of blue-red flame. As he traveled north through Italy, Dad kept seeing the same painting, but while George stayed about the same size, the dragon kept losing weight and getting smaller. In Germany he was down to the size of a Clydesdale. Finally, in Copenhagen, Dad couldn't believe his eyes. "That dragon still looked like a dragon, but the artist had shrunk him down to the size of a good-sized rabbit. Old George was holding him up by one ear, and I mean he couldn't have dressed out no more than four pounds, tops."

Then he wrapped it up. "The way I see it, South Carolina is about like Palermo. We have more imagination down here, and you know, bigger visions. You get north, up above Richmond, and it's like Copenhagen."

Along with this rich imagination, we also have the Gullah dialect, which is still heard down in the Low Country and out on the sea islands. Down here they still "read heads" and "work roots." They believe that "haint blue" and "haint green" painted on the doorjambs and window trims will keep the evil spirits away and that if you sweep your yard before the sun comes up, Doctor Death will keep on the other side of the road and go on about his business.

In Gullah, "he" stands for he, she, or it, and "um" stands for it, her, him, or them. Many of the words and phrases run on pure sound and cadence, and with the high-low jackrabbit delivery much of it sounds like calypso. If it sounds good, it is good. Proper names can be name brands, road signs, or a quick and clever riff from a new tune. One woman near Beaufort, who was named during the Kennedy funeral, proudly displays Cathedral Rotunda Johnson above the red birds on her rural delivery mailbox. And over near Fripp Island, the town of Pocotaligo is the compression of "poke a turtle's tail and he will go." Of the translatable Gullah proverbs and bromides, here are a fast few:

"Ef you play wid puppy, ee lick you face." (Familiarity breeds contempt.)

"Ef you ent hab hoss to ride, ride cow." (Half a loaf is better than none.)

"Po buckra an dog walk one pat." (The poor man and the dog walk the same path.)

If South Carolina looks like anything, it's a slice of pie that has not only been badly cut but lifted out of the pan much too early. Starting in the northwest corner at the Chattooga River—about the spot where Sheriff James Dickey, the late poet-in-residence at the University of South Carolina, leaned on his patrol car in the film *Deliverance*—the South Carolina–North Carolina line runs east for 333 rugged miles to Little River and the Atlantic Ocean. From Little River, the uninterrupted shoreline, with some of the best beaches in the country, stretches south more than 200 miles to Tybee Sound, only a few miles from Savannah, Georgia. From here up the wide Savannah River back to the northwest corner and the Chattooga, it's 240 miles.

Roughly paralleling the South Carolina coastline and running across the center of the state is another line—the fall line. This separates two distinct regions—the Upcountry and the Low Country, with the sandy Midlands in between. Most of the Upcountry is plateaus with rolling hills, ragged woods, fast-moving streams, and red-clay earth. First settled by Germans, Scots-Irish, and Welsh early in the eighteenth century, by 1800 the Upcountry had more than 30,000 small farmers who, with their self-sufficient way of life, had almost nothing in common with Low Country plantation owners. Today, while this region still has a great deal of farmland that produces soybeans, peaches, cotton, and tobacco, it is also a highly successful national and international manufacturing center. The giant BMW plant in Greenville is a notable example.

During the agricultural development of the Upcountry, the merchant-planters of the Low Country were living in the grand style of English gentlemen. Having named their first settlement Charles Town for England's King Charles II—the Merry Monarch who encouraged theater, horse racing, fine dining, dancing, and even golf—they were maintaining beautifully decorated town houses as well as sprawling and magnificent plantations and sending their children to London, Edinburgh, and Paris for their education.

Until only a few years ago, on East Bay Street in Charleston, the oldest printers in the South, Walker, Evans and Cogswell, knowing the precarious ways of the American dollar, still held onto their original Confederate money plates. Charlestonians are like this. They hold onto anything old: their houses, their furniture, their she-crab soup recipes, and their accents. It's this "holding-on" to the best aspects of the past and the sacred belief in landmarks that make Charleston possibly the most beautiful city in the country. With its low skyline and lantern-lit cobblestone streets, you can stroll along at night with a good domestic wine and a little imagination and find yourself in southern France or Ireland's County Kerry, or, for the more literary, the pages of Jane Austen.

Charlestonians also, despite earthquakes, hurricanes, plagues, and outright ridicule, cling to their family names with a desperation that approaches that of the American Kennel Club. If a young married lady is introducing herself she might admit that she is now unfortunately a Hampton. "I'm Elizabeth Moultrie Hampton." Then, with a perfectly sensible "south of Broad Street" change of key, she'll quickly add, "wuzza Heyward," letting you know there were cotillions and better days in the not-too-distant past.

I grew up in the Midlands 100 miles north of Charleston in Columbia. Every day on the way to school I could see the green-domed capitol of the State House and the bronze stars on the western side marking the spots where Sherman's shells had struck. They are still there and will probably be there forever. We grew up here with history all around us. In the old section of town, the streets are named for the Revolutionary generals Bull, Sumter, Pickens, and Marion. In the newer sections they bear the names of the Confederates: Lee, Jackson, Longstreet, Hampton, Pickett, and Green. In the section called "The Bottom," the names run the gamut from local politicians and famed prizefighters to attitudes and ambitions: Do Rite Alley, Easy Street, Sugar Ray Robinson Boulevard and Joe Louis Boulevard, and Captain Marvel Road (which is only 80 feet long and dead-ends into a trash pile). Everything else, from bridges and landfills to rest stops and runoff culverts, is named for the late Strom Thurmond.

In the small towns around Columbia, Greenville, and Spartanburg and on up to the North Carolina line, some traditions are set in stone and never change. The Atlantic coastline and the Southern tracks still gleam in the white gravel and the bright sun, and barefoot kids still walk the hot rails in the summertime. Fords, Chevys, and Plymouths, wrapped in honeysuckle and wisteria vines, still rust and rot out in the front yards and down in the drain ditches, and groups of three and four and five dogs still meet for all-night sessions under the streetlights at the crossroads.

We grew up here in the Midlands shooting squirrels in the swamp and carp in the river and rats at the trash pile. We sold iron to the iron man, paper to the paper man, and whiskey bottles to the bootleggers. We rode our bikes down the fifty or sixty or seventy steps of the State House, the courthouse, or whatever wedding-cake building was standing in the town square. We went to school here and joined the service here and came back from the service and went back to school here. Many of us left and went north or west or abroad, but almost all of us came back. Very few of us can put our finger on exactly why. Perhaps the best reason is that while we know it can get hot here in the summertime and pretty cool in the winter, the old Palmetto State is unlike any other place in the world.

Despite Hollywood's thigh-slapping, yee-hawing, chainsaw-dueling portrayal of South Carolinians, there is still a modicum of propriety and politeness down here not often found in the severe latitudes in the north. You will actually see men tip their hats to women and even give them their seats on the bus—there are no subways. And back in the smaller towns, suicides are toned down and usually reported as "after a short illness." But there are a few ground rules that you should know to make your trip here as easy and pleasant as possible.

Grits are served with all breakfasts. You can request home fries but don't be too surprised at what you get. Your best bet is to butter the grits, add pepper, mix them with your eggs, and not complain. An even better bet is to find a place that serves yellow grits instead of white—more on that later.

And contrary to what you've seen in the movies or read in the *National Enquirer,* there are no radar traps that track only northern license plates. The Highway Patrol officers are extremely helpful. If you have a flat tire or engine trouble, just sit back and wait. They'll come along and make all the arrangements for towing, tire changing, and so on. As a matter of fact, most of the Highway Patrol's time is spent doing precisely this. Many of them are very good shade-tree mechanics.

In the Low Country be careful driving during a heavy rainstorm. Especially in downtown Charleston, often the rain will come with a high tide, and the lower streets will flood with a mix of fresh and salt water that can ruin your car in minutes. Do not try to drive through this. Sit still until the water recedes, or leave the car and come back for it later, when it dries out.

Due to the fact that South Carolina has been one of the poorest states for so many years, the federal government has stepped in and built an excellent highway system. The four interstates—I–20, I–77, I–26, and I–95—that crisscross the state may very well be the best and smoothest in the country. We also have well-equipped and beautifully maintained rest stops. And like most of the rest of the country, you can turn right on a red light.

Sunday blue laws are too complicated to discuss in detail. Basically they assume that we all should be in church on Sunday and have no business shopping, drinking, or browsing through the malls from 8:00 a.m. to noon. Each county has its own laws, but most of

explodingafew southcarolina myths

A hoop snake will not put its tail in its mouth and roll down a hill.

A diamondback rattler will not wrap around your leg to hold you still while it bites. Now that would be scary!

A red fox will not run on three legs (resting a fourth) when running from the dogs.

Fire ants will not swarm over your legs and then, on a mysterious signal from their leader, bite you all at once. But don't try this one out. They can be absolutely savage and terrifying, and nothing short of a blowtorch can kill them.

South Carolina Food Specialties

Pimento cheese (Ruth's is the classic and can be found at most grocery stores.)

Boiled peanuts (Buy raw peanuts, stick them in a TON of water, with a TON of salt, approximately four cups worth, and boil until they look as if they've lost all integrity!)

Pickled boiled eggs

Pecan pie/sweet potato pie

Pepper jelly on cream cheese and crackers

Pork rinds (These can be bought in any store.)

them are now allowing stores, movies, and malls to open after noon. While you cannot buy beer or wine on Sunday, bars that have paid a stiff Sunday sales tax can be open on Sunday nights until midnight. All this will vary from county to county. Another blue law, called the Sundown Law, stipulates that you can't buy whiskey from a package store after the sun goes down. This law is in effect every night of the week. You can, however, buy wine and beer from almost any store.

A very helpful resource is the Parks, Recreation, and Tourism Board. Their phone number is (803) 734–0122, and they're open from 8:30 a.m. to 5:00 p.m. Monday through Friday. They can be contacted for free brochures and any and all information. Their Web site is www.scprt.com.

In South Carolina, everything happens on Labor Day. The football season opens, and in this part of the country, that's a religious experience in its own right. Across the sandhills and the Piedmont and on down the Congaree and the Cooper Rivers to Charleston, more than a hundred official barbecues, okra struts, catfish stomps, and demolition derbies all crank up at the same time. How to choose the best one is hard. But they're out there and all you have to do is check the papers or call the chambers of commerce.

Part of living in South Carolina and celebrating the survival of summer is the fall and the hundred fairs that crowd the calendars of the chambers of commerce. There are county fairs, town fairs, and fairs jimmied up at the crossroads with sawhorse tables for the pies and pickle relishes and rides that fold down from the backs of pickup trucks. The big one, the State Fair, is in Columbia in late September, and swirling around the centerpiece—a Saturn Rocket shipped up from Cape Canaveral—are more than 100,000 locals and not-so-locals eating elephant's ears, fried pies, and corn dogs, and then settling down to a first-class home-cooked meal in their favorite church tent while their kids ride everything from the Bumble Bee—for two-year-olds—to the Zipper, which after thirty years only the very young and the very drunk still ride.

South Carolina, with its own language, customs, and rhythms, is different. Very different. You'll see glimpses of it down on the coast in the shrimp boats and the oyster boats heading out at dawn and coming back in at dusk. You'll see it in the great blue heron as it glides across a marsh and settles under a moss-draped cypress tree, or in the possum—the small dog that doesn't bark—crossing a road carrying her litter. And you'll see it in that soft and sliding light at first dark that turns the roofs of Charleston from red to orange to gold to umber. I guess my dad was probably right; if we're like anything, we're like Palermo because, while we know that much of what we carry on about doesn't make a helluva lot of sense, we believe it anyway. In short, we have our own vision and version of history that works like this: It could have been, it should have been, it was. And in this happy delusion—sustained by azaleas in January and February, magnolias from March to August, gardenias, roses, wisteria, and 20-foot-high banana trees, fresh shrimp, and weather you can play golf in almost every day of the year—we still believe if Lee had had Jackson on his flank at Gettysburg, we could have won the day and the war, and the capital of these United States would be dead-center between Greenville 100 miles north and Charleston 100 miles south, right here in Columbia where it was originally scheduled to be. We also believe what one of our leaders proclaimed years ago: that while South Carolina is too small for a good-sized plantation and too big for an insane asylum, it's the only state in the nation that doesn't envy Virginia.

H. L. Mencken, no slouch with superlatives, went one better when he called the South Carolina lifestyle "a civilization of manifold excellences, perhaps the best the Western Hemisphere has ever seen."

That's pretty much the story on South Carolina from where I sit. These are some of the basic truths, anyway. I hope you enjoy yourself while traveling here in the Palmetto State. I really enjoyed putting this guidebook together on your behalf. But you need to be forewarned about something—South Carolina tends to grow on folks. They tend to swing back through here sooner rather than later when they start getting the wanderlust.

Here are a few more tidbits that may help make this information more useful as you go through the pages ahead. Restaurant cost categories refer to the price of entrees minus beverages, desserts, taxes, or tips. The ones I'd call "inexpensive" are $10 or less; "moderate" will run you somewhere between $10 and $15+; and "expensive" means $20 or more. Overnight accommodations listed as "inexpensive" are up to $100 per double per night; "moderate" are $101 to $200 per night, and "expensive" means you'll need to shell out $201 or more per night.

Here's to new adventures and the sweet, open road.

South Carolina Facts

- South Carolina was the eighth state to sign the Constitution and the first state to secede from the Union before the Civil War. Edisto Island, south of Charleston, decreed that if the state didn't secede, it would secede from South Carolina.
- South Carolina grows more peaches than any other state except California.
- South Carolina has one of the oldest formal gardens in America—Middleton Gardens, finished in 1740.
- South Carolina has 187 miles of coastline and arguably the best beaches in America. On some beaches you won't see a single soul for more than a mile, even in the middle of summer.
- On a hot day, kudzu can grow more than a foot. Some teachers string it across the outside of a window so the pupils can actually watch it grow.

South Carolina State Symbols

- **State Tree**—Palmetto Tree
- **State Nickname**—The Palmetto State
- **State Animal**—White-tailed Deer
- **State Game Bird**—Wild Turkey
- **State Fish**—Striped Bass
- **State Reptile**—Loggerhead Turtle
- **State Insect**—Praying Mantis
- **State Butterfly**—Eastern Tiger Swallowtail
- **State Dog**—Boykin Spaniel
- **State Bird**—Carolina Wren
- **State Flower**—Yellow Jessamine
- **State Motto**—"Prepared in mind and resources. While I breathe, I hope."

Charleston and the Surrounding Area

Downtown Charleston

Charleston, which has been called The Holy City; The City by the Sea, Where the Ashley and the Cooper Rivers Meet to Form the Atlantic Ocean; and The Home of Rhett Butler, is the perfect place to begin a tour of the old Palmetto State. Settled in 1680, this remarkable town literally has to be seen to be believed.

My grandmother, who was from the Midlands around Columbia, used to huff and hiss, "Charlestonians are all right but everybody knows they're just too poor to paint and too proud to whitewash." That used to be true. Not any more. One look at the real estate prices and you'll see how much that's all changed.

You might consider seriously the recommendation that you don't even think about driving around Charleston. The streets are narrow, some are paved with cobblestones, and the one-way traffic can be a nightmare in rush hours. (Women wearing high heels will have a tough time negotiating cobblestones.) Parking on the street is almost impossible. The easier approach is to park your car in a downtown lot or the visitor center and forget it. The standard rate is about $8.00 a day.

Since Charleston and the Low Country area attract more than five million guests each year, hotel, guest house, and bed-and-breakfast owners have built a reputation for hospitality and extremely high standards. Charleston is famous for its bed-and-breakfasts in particular, and one local service does everything possible to match the guests to whatever sort of accommodations they want: Historic Charleston Bed and Breakfast (843–722–6606 or 800–743–3583; www .historiccharlestonbedandbreakfast.com).

Some bed-and-breakfasts provide bicycles that will help you get around the city on tours of your own arrangement. Lodgings in these homes and inns provide the wonderful feeling that you are staying in the very heart of the old city like a true Charlestonian. Listed below are a few that are off the beaten path yet have all the amenities for an enjoyable, comfortable stay.

Battery Carriage House Inn at 20 South Battery. Rates range from $150 to $299, and include continental breakfast, wine and cheese in the evening, and turn-down service. The majority of the rooms are off a side garden but you're steps away from Charleston's famous Battery and White Point Gardens. The rooms are furnished in period reproductions. Each room has its own private bath as well as separate air-conditioning and heating controls. Call (843) 727–3100, (800) 775–5575, or visit www.batterycarriagehouse.com.

Lowndes Grove Plantation, 266 Margaret Street, offers a bed-and-breakfast experience that's clearly off the beaten path from the Battery, as mentioned above. Yet this is an authentic Ashley River plantation house and

AUTHOR'S FAVORITE PLACES

Angel Oak
(843) 559–3496

The Battery
At the tip of the Charleston peninsula

Best Friend Bar at The Mills House
115 Meeting Street

Boone Hall
(843) 884–4371
www.boonehallplantation.com

The Calhoun Mansion
16 Meeting Street
(843) 722–8205

Charleston Country Club
(843) 406–0895

Dock Street Theatre
(843) 720–3968
www.charlestonstage.com

Middleton Place
4300 Ashley River Road
(843) 556–6020 or (800) 782–3608
www.middletonplace.org

Ocean Course at Kiawah
(843) 768–2121 or (800) 654–2924
www.kiawahisland.com

St. Michael's Episcopal Church
Corner of Meeting and Broad Streets
(843) 723–0603
www.stmichaelschurch.org

one that's actually within the city limits. The house, built about 1786, and its landscaped grounds give guests a rural feeling of open space, spectacular gardens, and fabulous views of the historic river itself. This house once hosted President Theodore Roosevelt when it was part of the 1901 West Indies Exhibition at nearby Hampton Park. Six air-conditioned guest rooms (priced from $100 to $200) plus a costlier guest cottage all have enormous antebellum charm. Continental breakfast is served daily. Call (843) 723–8438 or visit www .lowndesgrove.com.

Here's how you might begin a Charleston tour. Make *The Mills House* on the corner of Meeting and Queen your starting point. It's located in the very center of the old town. Then try a walking tour of a few spots close by. Several tours depart from there or close by. Or, you can go it alone following this guide. If you can, spend a night or two at The Mills. It's a beautiful restoration of what it was before the Civil War. As a matter of fact, on the second floor you can stand on the wrought-iron balcony where in 1861 Robert E. Lee stood and watched much of the old town burn.

The 215-room hotel is located at 115 Meeting Street and has accommodations that range from $150 to suites at $369; parking available at no extra charge. It has an outdoor swimming pool on the third floor with a very comfortable sundeck where you can get a cool drink and a light snack. The *Best Friend Bar* on the lobby floor, with very good local musical talent, is the perfect spot after a night on the town. Across the beautiful marble lobby is the recently refurbished *Barbados Room,* which has earned the Mobil Travel Guide four-star award. Here they serve breakfast, lunch, and a romantic candlelit dinner. The evening menu is expensive, but worth it. The Sunday brunch there is fantastic. Before you dine, be sure to sip a drink in the fountain courtyard. For reservations and information, call (843) 577–2400 or visit www .millshouse.com.

The Mills House

Still using The Mills House as a starting point, you can cross Meeting and walk exactly one block down Queen to Church to one of the oldest and most charming operating playhouses in the country, *The Dock Street Theatre.* The original theater, built in 1735, has long vanished, but the 1800s hotel built on the site was converted into a theater in 1935, by the Works Progress Administration (WPA). During Spoleto, the seventeen-day annual music and art festival held in Charleston in late May and early June, the theater is the centerpiece for chamber music and plays. A few years back, one of Arthur Miller's last plays premiered here.

The Dock Street Theatre is currently undergoing a major face-lift, but you might catch it open for tours and individual browsing from 10:00 a.m. to 4:00 p.m. Monday through Friday unless a rehearsal is under way. The building, which has been reconstructed over and over again, handsomely captures the Georgian architecture that flourished during that period. Dock Street seats 463 and has a pit and a parquet of thirteen boxes. Over the stage is a carved wood bas-relief of the Royal Coat of Arms of England. The cove ceiling has exceptional acoustic properties—when string quartets perform here during the Spoleto Festival, any seat in the house is a good seat.

The old theater plays a leading role in the intellectual and cultural life of the city. All year long the theater features dramas, musicals, and family fare, as well as readings and recitals. Late May and early June are booked solid with concerts and plays during the Spoleto Festival. Call (843) 720–3968 for information or visit www.charlestonstage.com.

A block and a half back up Queen and past The Mills House is *82 Queen,* a combination oyster bar, stand-up brass-railed pub, and fine restaurant. The building, formerly two adjoining nineteenth-century town houses, has a lovely courtyard dining area complete with awnings, umbrellas, and banks of shrubbery. Specialties here are seafood, beef, and fowl, with prices ranging from $12 to $25. The bar, which fronts on Queen, is a notorious hangout for local authorities on everything from ornithology to transcendentalism, and if you listen long enough you will probably hear it all. One local sage, deep in the grape, cornered me not too long ago with the red-hot, ice-cold information that Charleston inbreeding, which rivals that of the ancient Egyptians, has been going on so long and with such intensity that there isn't an empty attic on the whole peninsula. Call (843) 722–4428 or go to www.82queen.com.

A few doors back up Queen at number 72 is *Poogan's Porch,* which serves gumbos, jambalayas, and great crab cakes. The bread pudding and peanut butter pie are especially good and have become a tradition here on Queen. You can eat indoors or out on the veranda. For lunch, stay inside with the air-conditioning. For dinner, when it cools off, it's nice to eat outside. The

The Elizabeth O'Neill
Verner home

name Poogan came from the dog who was left behind when the original owner sold the house and moved away. Since then the restaurant has changed hands several times, but each time the dog remained behind as the mascot until he died in 1979. Poogan's is open every day for lunch and dinner. Prices range from $15 to $22. Call (843) 577–2337 or check out www.poogansporch.com.

From Poogan's Porch go back to The Mills House and follow Meeting Street south to 38 Tradd Street. Turn left here and walk one block to 38 Tradd Street. This was the home of the painter Elizabeth O'Neill Verner (1883–1979), internationally famous for her pen-and-ink drawings and paintings of the Charleston skyline, its churches, and the local flower ladies and basket weavers. Prints of her work are on exhibit and for sale exclusively at the Gibbes Museum of Art Shop at 135 Meeting Street, just north of the Mills House. Verner's drawings and paintings are quintessentially Charleston and are not to be missed.

Directly behind 38 Tradd Street at 91 Church Street is **Cabbage Row.** Originally four or five connected buildings around a central courtyard, today it is a boutique featuring designer clothing, gifts, jewelry, and a wide variety of accessories. It was here that Porgy of DuBose Heyward's book of that name lived. "Cabbage Row" was changed to "Catfish Row" for DuBose Heyward and George Gershwin's folk opera *Porgy and Bess.* In 1934 Gershwin spent a summer in Charleston and lived a few miles away on Folly Beach where he and Heyward collaborated on the now world-famous opera set in Charleston. Most of the staging was based on the courtyard, and much of Gershwin's inspiration for the score came from the sounds of the neighborhood street vendors (the strawberry man, the butter bean man, and the fresh shrimp man).

Many of the letters of Gershwin to his brother Ira in New York describe life in Charleston in the 1930s and the devastation he witnessed from a hurricane. They also reveal a curious downside to the famous composer. Gershwin, hell-bent on self-promotion, tried to get the Charlestonians to rename Folly Beach as Gershwin Island. Fortunately Charlestonians knew where to draw the line and Folly Beach is still Folly Beach. These letters are available for reading in the South Carolina room of the Charleston Public Library at 68 Calhoun Street.

If you're a football, baseball, basketball, or golf fan and can't stand missing too much of the action, make a note of the ***Charleston Crab House*** at 41 South Market Street. A wide variety of sandwiches and beverages is available here with a large TV screen carrying all the sports action. Prices are $4.00 to $7.00. Call (843) 853–2900 or visit www.charlestoncrabhouse.com.

On King Street about a block from The Mills House is one of the most elegant and tasteful women's clothing shops on the entire East Coast. Its name, ***R.T.W.,*** means ready-to-wear, and the place and the selections will make you ready to buy. Once you've tried something on and closed your eyes to the price, you'll probably want to wear it right then and there.

Jan McMenamin is the owner, and she has a marvelous eye for fashion and what particular women need to match their skin tone, eyes, hair, and anything else that needs matching. As a matter of fact, she often goes abroad for a small group of her favorite customers and buys whatever she sees that she knows will please them. She is seldom, if ever, wrong. If you're in a quandary about what you should wear and how you should wear it, see her. For the nervous spouse fingering his credit card, Jan serves complimentary wine, brandy, coffee, tea, and an assortment of local sweets. You can park at the side of the store or one block away at the city parking lot right behind The Mills House. Even if you don't buy anything, go in and look around—it's a one of a kind. Call (843) 577–9748 or check out www.rtwcharleston.com.

Charleston Place, located at 205 Meeting Street, is one of the premier hotels in the South. Off the beautiful lobby is a small but fine selection of stores including Talbots, Godiva, Laura Ashley, Gucci, and Doubleday Books. The lounge at the hotel is elegant, and while the musicians who play there change frequently, they are all very, very good. Room rates begin at about $200. Dinners range from $30 to $50 and up. Call (843) 722–4900 or go to www.charlestonplacehotel.com. It's not altogether "off the beaten path," but it's a place where you should at least drop in for a glass of something.

Hyman's Seafood at 215 Meeting Street next to the Omni Hotel, has been voted the number one seafood restaurant in town. They serve fifteen to twenty-five different fish any way you like, as well as shellfish, aged beef, and several pasta dishes. Hyman's specializes in frying with olive oil, and their seafood can be had broiled, fried, or blackened. The okra soup is especially delicious and different. They're open seven days a week from 11:00 a.m. to 11:00 p.m. Prices range from $10.95 to $21.95. If you're driving, which you shouldn't be, park in the Omni Hotel garage next door. Call (843) 723–6000 or visit www.hymansseafood.com.

Spoleto Festival USA
(last week in May, first week in June)

The Calhoun Mansion at 16 Meeting Street is much more than a house, and a tour of this extravaganza is well worth the price of admission. To begin, it is 24,000 square feet (the average family home is approximately 3,000 square feet). Built in 1876, this privately owned Victorian showplace is divided into twenty-five rooms, each with different and elaborate tile floors and ornamental plaster molding. The ballroom, with its skylight and 45-foot-high ceiling, is the centerpiece. The furnishings and artwork are eclectic and as unusual as the house itself. For instance, on the second floor is a great surprise for the children—a 14-foot stuffed and rampaging polar bear. One of the best-known movie-making secrets is the fact that the Calhoun Mansion was featured in the television miniseries *North and South* as the Pennsylvania home of the Hazzards. If you meet the right people at 82 Queen or The Best Friend Bar at The Mills House, you might get a sunset tour of the roof of the old mansion, which may be the most beautiful view in all of Charleston. Open daily 10:00 a.m. to 4:00 p.m. Admission is $15 per person; children under six are admitted free. Call (843) 722–8205.

After leaving the Calhoun Mansion, stroll up to the corner of Meeting and Broad, a junction known as *The Four Corners of Law.* Here you'll see the flower ladies, whom Elizabeth O'Neill Verner so lovingly painted, selling daisies, daffodils, or whatever is in season. Most of them are also basket ladies. If you're lucky, you'll hear them singing as they weave their ancient patterns from sweet grass, pine needles, and bulrushes and bind their elaborate work together with fiber strips from palmetto trees. The baskets, which come in a variety of shapes and sizes, are truly unique and can only be purchased here and out on Route 17 heading north. They last for generations and make wonderful presents.

After this little excursion, which should give you a feeling for the old town, your next best stop is *The Charleston Visitor Reception and Transportation Center* at 375 Meeting Street. One of the best visitor centers in the country, it can save you time, money, and especially shoe leather if you decide to go on the walking tours. Its gracious and well-informed attendants can help you with almost everything, including tours, lodging, restaurants, parking, attractions, and entertainment.

Built in 1856, the visitor center is a redbrick, high-ceilinged building that was formerly the Railroad Depot. Large-scale maps along with old photos and prints illustrate how the city has changed and developed since 1670, when the first English settlers anchored here and came ashore. Computerized maps equipped with video stations are also available. You can call up information on interactive screens and request additional advice on direct-line telephones. A service counter with helpful attendants is at your disposal and is a central location for obtaining tour and theater tickets.

A twenty-minute show entitled *Forever Charleston* is a combination of slides, music, city sounds, and narration by Charlestonians. Shown every half hour, it is a beautifully photographed production but seems long on charm and short on story, insight, and humor. It also needs a cleaner sound track. Nonetheless, buy a couple of pecan pralines from the attendant—they are delicious—and see it anyway. The tidewater panoramas and heron, egret, and alligator shots are worth the $2.50 admission and will get you in the perfect mood for touring the incredible homes, gardens, and plantations around the old city. The center is open from 8:30 a.m. to 5:30 p.m. daily but closes a half hour earlier in November, December, and February. It is also closed on Thanksgiving, Christmas, and New Year's Day. Call (843) 853–8000 or (800) 868–8118, or go to www.charlestoncvb.com.

Next door to the visitor center, you'll find a depot for the **Downtown Area Shuttles (DASH),** which leave every fifteen minutes for tours through different sections of Charleston. DASH shuttles for tourists are the green "trolleys," different from the CARTA mass-transit buses. One-way tickets are $1.25; a daylong pass is only $4.00. A good bet is to take several rides so you can figure out what area of town you'd like to explore by foot or horse-drawn carriage ride. Many people make the DASH depot their first stop, parking their cars here and taking a few quick rides in the shuttles before deciding where they would like to stay. For more on DASH and CARTA, go to www.ridecarta .com.

If you head back toward The Mills House Hotel from the visitor center along Meeting Street, you'll find yourself approaching the white brick Days Inn motel on the right at 155 Meeting Street. What would otherwise be the motel's rather expected restaurant, attached to the complex just off the parking lot, is actually an independent eatery called **Diana's.** Well, Diana's is anything but expected. In fact, this may be one of the best-kept secrets in Charleston. The food is relatively inexpensive, as the peninsula restaurants go, and that's your first break. Then, the portions are enormous and the cooking is truly fine. If you're anywhere near here at breakfast time, you must try her apple French toast. The portobello "burger" is a delight for lunch, and there's an array of dinner specials every night. The dessert kiosk filled with pies and cakes is beyond temptation. They even have a small cocktail bar for "happy hour" or a cold beer on a hot day. Diana's opens at 6:30 a.m. for those who want to get an early start on discovering Charleston. Dinner reservations are suggested, as the seating is limited, and Diana's secret is getting out. Call (843) 534–0043 or check out the list of specials posted on the chalkboard outside.

boiledpeanuts

Look for and buy a sack of boiled peanuts, then see what happens. At first you will be repulsed by their appearance—they're brown and soft and look very, very suspicious. But get over it and try three or four. By the fourth or fifth, you will be hooked for life, and when you head back north you'll be loaded down with them. Unfortunately, like South Carolina peaches and sweet corn, they don't travel well and have to be shelled and eaten as close to the patch as you can get. You can buy them right on the street.

From Diana's, it's only a block farther south to the **Gibbes Museum of Art** at 135 Meeting Street. Open Tuesday through Saturday from 10:00 a.m. to 5:00 p.m., Sunday 1:00 to 5:00 p.m, closed Monday. Admission is $7.00 for adults, $6.00 for seniors and college students, $4.00 for children ages six to eighteen. Considered one of the best collections in the entire Southeast, this museum exhibits 500 eighteenth- and nineteenth-century portraits as well as sculpture and Japanese wood-block prints. The gift shop has a wonderful collection of note cards, postcards, and books that make excellent gifts. Don't be afraid to bring the kids here; there is plenty to keep them amused and busy. Call (843) 722–2706 or visit www .gibbesmuseum.org.

In case you've forgotten, this is a seaport and a haven for boaters of all stripes. Same goes for hunters and fishermen (and fisherwomen, too). Just off Calhoun at 78 Alexander Street is **Luden's,** a sportsman's delight if ever there was one. Since 1867, they've been selling Charlestonians their top-quality clothing for hunting, fishing, and boating plus all the gear to go with it. This is a great source for gift items for the outdoor enthusiasts in your life as well. Tide clocks, ship's logs, nautical charts, cookbooks for boaters, fly rods, oyster knives—you name it, they've got it. It's a little hard to find, though. Alexander Street is a block off East Bay, near the back of the Charleston County Library. Call (843) 723–7829 or visit www.ludensoutfitter.com.

For the budget minded, only a few blocks away—we're still walking— you'll find **Jestine's Kitchen** at 251 Meeting Street. The specialties here are Low Country home cooking, vegetables, fish, and really wonderful fried chicken. The price range is from $7.00 to $15.00. Open from 11:00 a.m. to 9:30

p.m. Tuesday through Thursday, 11:00 a.m. to 10:00 p.m. Friday and Saturday, 11:00 a.m. to 9:00 p.m. Sunday, closed Monday. Call (843) 722–7224.

On the other hand, you can go to **S.N.O.B.** at 192 East Bay Street for exquisite dining and an equally exquisite atmosphere. The tongue-in-cheek acronym officially stands for its location, "Slightly North of Broad." The specialty here is Low Country cooking along with a number of very fine continental dishes. One of the local favorites is shrimp and yellow grits. Prices range from $17 to $30 and wine is served. Lunch is served from 11:30 a.m. to 3:00 p.m., dinner from 5:30 to 10:00 p.m. While down south, try to get yellow grits rather than white. There's a big, big difference—the yellow are not over-processed and have a much better taste. You can even buy them, although only in some stores. Call S.N.O.B. at (843) 723–3424 or see www.slightlynorthofbroad.net.

In the South Windemere Shopping Center, at 90 Folly Road, you'll find the Mediterranean Delicatessen or **Med Deli.** Their specialties are pasta, seafood, sandwiches, and dinners, priced from $7.00 to $12.00, along with a huge wholesale arrangement for buying wine. The Med is open from 11:00 a.m. to 10:00 p.m. Monday through Saturday and serves lunch ($4.00 to $6.00) until 2:00 p.m. Closed Sunday. Call (843) 766–0323.

Vickerys, at 15 Beaufain, serves Cuban food and Low Country cuisine, as well as excellent seafood. This is a big and busy place and has a nice outdoor seating arrangement. Open daily, 11:30 to 1:00 a.m. Price range here is $10 to $20. Wine is available. Call (843) 577–5300 or go to www.vickerysbarandgrill.com.

On up the street from The Mills House is **the Joseph Manigault House** at 350 Meeting Street. This classic example of the graceful Adam style was designed and built by the architect Gabriel Manigault in 1803. The graceful, elliptical staircase, which you will also see in the *Forever Charleston* show back at the visitor center, is the centerpiece. In the 1920s the place was a broken-down boarding house, and for a while in the 1930s it was a service station. The dean of the Harvard School of Architecture and a number of Charlestonians took it upon themselves to help restore and furnish it with the period furniture you see here today. This is one of the few houses in Charleston that still has a gatehouse. Open 10:00 a.m. to 5:00 p.m. Monday through Saturday and 1:00 to 5:00 p.m. Sunday. Last tour is at 4:30 p.m. Admission is $8.00 for adults and $4.00 for children three to twelve. Call (843) 723–2926 or contact the Charleston Museum at (843) 722–2996 for combination tickets to all of the museum sites. Their Web site is www.charlestonmuseum.org.

For one of the best views, you simply have to visit the **Rooftop Terrace Bar at The Library at Vendue Inn,** located at 19 Vendue Range. This popular spot offers a charming view of the churches and many of the old tile roofs and quaint chimneys of the old city. The cuisine here is distinctly southern, and everybody who comes here just keeps coming back. Full dinners cost around $30. Call (843) 577–7970 or (800) 845–7900. Open seven days a week from 5:00 to 10:00 p.m. Visit www.vendueinn.com.

The *Nathaniel Russell House,* located at 51 Meeting Street, is another showcase home and a Charleston favorite. Spacious gardens surround this old house, recognized as one of America's finest examples of neoclassical architecture. Its elaborate plasterwork ornamentation, its free-flying staircase rising up through three complete stories without any visible means of support, and its beautiful proportions prompted the celebrated French aristocrat Henry Deas Lesesne to proclaim it to be "beyond all comparison the finest establishment in Charleston." Open Monday through Saturday 10:00 a.m. to 5:00 p.m. and Sunday from 2:00 until 5:00 p.m. Admission is $8.00 for adults. Children under six are admitted free. Call (843) 724–8481 or see www.historiccharleston.org.

Lodge Alley at 195 East Bay Street is a place that anyone who has the slightest interest in renovation shouldn't miss. A dozen years ago this was an ugly string of decaying warehouses. Today it is a beautiful inn with a fountain in the center court and an excellent restaurant. The specialties at the restaurant are roast squab and rack of lamb, as well as seafood and Low Country cuisine. If you don't stay here or eat here, at least stop by for a drink at the small, intimate bar overlooking the courtyard, but beware of time share salespeople lurking about. Call (843) 722–1611 or visit www.bluegreenrentals.com.

Gaulart and Maliclet at 98 Broad Street, in the heart of the city, prides itself on being fast and French. They are just that—and given the high quality of their food and fine service, surprisingly economical. I had a cup of delicious split-pea soup, a sandwich of pâté and blue cheese, and excellent coffee for around $6.00. They have a very fine wine list; but best of all, their steady customers all seem remarkably upbeat and happy and seem to know one another. This is one of the smallest eateries in town. But it's also one of the really very fine Charleston surprises. It's a great place to drop in for lunch or dinner and sit at the bar and listen to the music and the local gossip. Open 8:30 a.m. to 4:00 p.m. Monday, 8:00 a.m. to 10:00 p.m. Tuesday through Thursday, and 8:00 a.m. to 4:00 p.m. Friday and Saturday. Call (843) 577–9797.

Put this one on the very top of your list: *Robert's of Charleston Dinner Restaurant* at 182 East Bay Street. Call (843) 577–7565 or (800) 977–7565 or go to www.robertsofcharleston.com. Save up a few bucks, shore up your appetite, and take your sweetheart here. It will be the best money you've spent in a long, long time. Billed as "Charleston's most romantic restaurant," it's far more than that. The centerpiece is one of the most extraordinary characters on the peninsula, Robert Dickson. Not only is he the remarkable host of one of the best restaurants on the *entire coast* but he's also a wonderful singer, from

Puccini to German Leider to every song you can remember from Broadway shows. Every few years he takes a group of very lucky Charlestonians to Italy, where they visit the great eating establishments, and Robert takes requests and sings to them before, during, and after the meals. I have a close friend who went with him the last time and plans to go again and again for the rest of his life. Recently, Robert Dickson pulled off an event we'll be talking about forever. He invited two full Tuscany choirs—a grand total of thirty-one people—to entertain the lucky diners at the restaurant. The two choirs had already given performances at St. Michael's Church and Alumni Hall at the University of Charleston. At Robert's restaurant they divided up into four groups and sang secular Renaissance music a cappella. The performance was spellbinding. So stop by, meet Robert Dickson, and at least have a glass of wine. There's no telling what he will be up to next. Dinner at Robert's for his five-course, prix fixe meal is $75. This is quite a sight, so don't dare be late.

Gardens and Historic Plantations

Not only is there a lot to see and do in Charleston, there is a great deal just outside the city limits on the barrier islands—namely, Isle of Palms, Sullivan's Island, Seabrook, and Kiawah. South of Charleston on Route 17, the Savannah Highway, you'll see the sign for Seabrook and Kiawah Islands. Turn here on Main Road to Bohicket Road and proceed exactly 7.3 miles to the sign for **Angel Oak** and turn right. The sandy road will look deserted (because it is), and you'll think you're on the wrong road. But stay with it for about a half mile and you'll see a sight you will never, ever forget—the Angel Oak. It's one of the true American wonders. Don't forget your camera for this one. Best of all, admission is free. Call (843) 559–3496 for more information.

The Angel Oak may be the oldest living thing east of the Mississippi River—estimated at more than 1,400 years old. A few Angel Oak specifics: height 65 feet; circumference 25.5 feet; area of shade 17,000 square feet; largest limb circumference 11.25 feet; largest limb length 89 feet. In other words, it has to be seen to be believed.

In the opposite direction, 14 miles northwest of Charleston on Route 61, is the site of America's oldest landscaped garden, at **Middleton Place,** 4300 Ashley River Road, Charleston. The plantation was laid out on the banks of the Ashley River, and the grounds include a fascinating museum house in a restored flanker to the original mansion, a modern inn, and one of the world's most beautiful gardens.

A recent addition to the exhibits at Middleton is an actual freedman's dwelling, furnished as it was in the 1870s when it was lived in by freed slaves who stayed on the plantation after the emancipation. You will also see blacksmiths, potters, weavers, and carpenters who will explain and demonstrate what they are doing and tell you about the plantation's history. The main house was built in 1741 but was burned by Union troops in 1865. As the story goes, the soldiers drank wine and had a glorious dinner with heavy silver and fancy linen at the main house, then they set fire to it and left.

Perhaps the best part of Middleton Place is the incredible view from the high terraces of the azalea, camellia, and rose gardens that roll down the hill into the Butterfly Lakes. The restaurant here serves authentic Low Country dishes for lunch and they prepare a wonderful candlelight dinner. The gift shop sells plantation-crafted wares, books, and fine gifts for discerning guests. During the Spoleto Festival, Middleton often serves as the site for the grand finale. With the Spoleto Orchestra playing on a stage built over the Butterfly Lakes against a backdrop of fireworks, the huge crowd sits on blankets under the stars. What a concert! Open daily from 9:00 a.m. to 5:00 p.m. Call (843) 556–6020 or (800) 782–3608 or see www.middletonplace.org.

Continuing on Route 61, turn right at Route 165 and in a few miles you'll come to *Summerville,* one of the most charming towns in the South. Formerly a winter resort for Charlestonians and Columbians, its streets ramble in curves through the trees. The lavish blooms of azaleas, camellias, and wisteria glow against the dark background of pines. Small boys still rush out to your car if they suspect you're a tourist, holding up signs marked GUIDE. Only two blocks from the business section is the Azalea Park and Bird Sanctuary. More than 800 specimens of native plants grow in the park. In the winter thousands of migratory birds stop here on their way south. This is a delightful town, and you will see not only enormous areas covered with azaleas and camellias but also hedges and ornamental shrubs of tea plants. Back in 1890 Dr. Charles U. Shepard began experimentation in commercial tea growing, and for a short time Lipton Tea helped finance his enterprise. His farm eventually failed, but the growing of tea for commercial purposes has resurfaced recently on nearby Wadmalaw Island. The knowledge of planting tea lived on in Summerville and can be seen all over town in the hedges and ornamental shrubs. Incidentally, the tea plant is a close cousin of the camellia.

Heading back toward Charleston on Route 61, about 5 miles after passing Middleton Place again, you will see *Magnolia Plantation and Gardens,* at 3550 Ashley River Road. The 300-year-old plantation is the ancestral home of South Carolina's illustrious Drayton family; ten generations have used it since 1670. Internationally famous, it is considered to be one of America's oldest man-made attractions. Noted for its springtime beauty, it features more than

250 varieties of azalea and 900 varieties of camellia, as well as beautiful seasonal blooms every month of the year.

This is an ideal place for the kids. You can paddle a canoe through the waterways of the 125-acre waterfowl refuge or view it from a wildlife observation tower along its walkways. Children will also enjoy Magnolia's rare minihorses, as well as its petting zoo where the kids can feed and pet a score of animals. Even your pets are welcome here—as long as they stay on a leash. An interesting addition at Magnolia in the wildlife preserve is The Audubon Swamp Garden, which is sixty acres of black water in a cypress and tupelo swamp. The garden is accessible via boardwalks and dikes and is home to every species of Low Country wildlife. To reach Magnolia Gardens from Charleston, drive 10 miles west on Route 61. You'll see the signs. Magnolia Gardens is open 8:00 a.m. to 5:30 p.m. every day. Admission is $14.00 for adults and teenagers, $8.00 for children ages six to twelve, and free for children under age six. Call (843) 571–1266 or (800) 367–3517. Visit www.magnoliaplantation.com.

Birds of Prey

If you see a hawk, eagle, owl, vulture, falcon, kite, or osprey—any raptor—on the side of the road that has been hit by a car and is in trouble, *there is something you can do about it.* Wrap the bird up in a towel and place it in a dark box or trunk if it's not too hot. You must keep it out of the light. Then call the **South Carolina Center for Birds of Prey** at (843) 928–3494. Or, you may go to www.internationalbirdsofprey.org for more information. They will arrange for you to drop it off at a convenient place where their staff, or one of their countless volunteers, will pick it up and take it to their headquarters on Route 17 north of Charleston. As a matter of fact, if you are in some state other than South Carolina, you can still call that number or visit that Web site and they will give you the number of the nearest Birds of Prey Recovery Hospital.

The center, founded by Jim Singleton of Charleston, is a modern, well-equipped hospital owned and supported by tax-free contributions only and

Facts about Raptors

A red-tailed hawk, if it could read, could read the *New York Times* from a mile away. It can also kill a full-sized crow by merely squeezing it with its talons.

An owl can swivel its head 270 degrees.

An osprey, if it finds that you can see into its nest, will build it higher.

An osprey carries fish with the head forward and the tail behind to limit drag.

is probably one of the finest and best-managed in the entire Southeast. When they receive an injured bird, they quickly X-ray it to find out the damage, then they set the bones, treat it, and place it in a holding area where in most cases it recovers. Every year they treat and release more than 200 raptors.

A couple of years ago, they reset a bald eagle's wing and kept him in their holding building for weeks to make sure the wing had healed properly. I was there when they released it, and I'm here to say it was a sight to see. First of all, the bird had a wingspan of 5 to 6 feet, and when it took off, you could see the pine straw and the leaves on the ground move and you could feel the breeze. He flew to a pine tree limb about a hundred yards away, took a long look around to get his bearings, said his good-byes, and headed out for Colorado—where he was probably from. For smaller birds that are injured, I guess the best bet is the Audubon Society. Oh, and what happens to birds that recover and still can't fly away? These birds are given a happy home right here and are used in educational projects throughout the state.

In the general area of Magnolia Plantation and Gardens and Middleton Place along Highway 171, between Interstate 26 and Route 17, you will find ***Charles Towne Landing State Historical Site.*** This is where you'll find the first permanent English settlement in the state and the birthplace of South Carolina. Today this newly refurbished and freshly interpreted park is preserved as a national treasure—a one-of-a-kind state park filled with history and natural splendor. The Landing is also a great place for children. Here they can see the *Adventure,* a full-scale replica of a seventeenth-century trading vessel in its dry dock being restored. They can explore eighty acres of lush gardens or walk through the winding trails of the natural habitat zoo, which features wolves, puma, bears, and bison. A hands-on activities exhibit for the kids uses household tools and crafts common in the seventeenth century. For further information contact Charles Towne Landing, 1500 Old Town Road, Charleston, 29407, or call (843) 852–4200. Check out www.southcarolinaparks .com.

If you're still in a visiting-a-garden mood after you've visited Magnolia Plantation and Gardens, you're only 12 miles from ***Cypress Gardens,*** a 162-acre swamp garden created in the 1920s and festooned with flower-lined pathways. Each spring a profusion of azaleas, dogwood, daffodils, and wisteria is reflected in the mirrors of the black waters. Outdoor enthusiasts and bird-watchers will particularly enjoy the two rambling nature trails here, which wind through habitats and nesting areas for the alligator, pileated woodpecker, river otter, barred owl, and wood duck. You can explore the gardens in the traditional manner, with a guided flat-bottomed boat tour, or you can rent a canoe and paddle yourself off the beaten trail to who knows where.

From Charleston take Interstate 26 to exit 208 (Moncks Corner). Follow Highway 52 north a couple of miles and watch for signs to Cypress Gardens. Open February through December. Admission for adults is $10.00, seniors pay $9.00, children six through twelve pay $5.00, and children under six are admitted free. Call (843) 553–0515 or visit www.cypressgardens.org.

And finally, one more plantation! ***Boone Hall*** is the one everyone wants to see—the plantation that was featured in the TV miniseries *North and South*. The entrance alone, through two magnificent columns of eighty-eight live oaks, is worth the price of admission. Captain Thomas Boone planted one hundred live oaks in 1743, and, amazingly enough, eighty-eight have survived. Visitors can tour the (ca. 1930s) Greek Revival–style mansion and walk through the azalea and camellia gardens. Nine original slave cabins from the eighteenth century are also here. Boone Hall is 8 miles north of Charleston on Route 17 at 1235 Long Point Road, Mount Pleasant. Admission is $14.50 for adults, $13.00 for senior citizens, and $7.00 for children ages six through twelve. Children under six are admitted free. Open all year. April through Labor Day, hours are 8:30 a.m. to 6:30 p.m. daily except Sunday, when hours are 1:00 to 5:00 p.m. Open the rest of the year from 9:00 a.m. to 5:00 p.m. daily, except Sunday, when hours are 1:00 to 4:00 p.m. Call (843) 884–4371 or see www.boonehallplantation.com.

Crossing over the Cooper River Bridge, you'll find the popular ***Shem Creek Bar and Grill*** at 508 Mill Street, Mount Pleasant, where they pride themselves on "cookin' on the Creek." This is the home of Sloppy John's Oyster Bar and Dock. Shem's is also accessible by water, and boats park right at the bar. They specialize in grilled seafood and beef, served indoors or outdoors on the "gazebos" overlooking Shem Creek. The place is big and at times noisy, but it has a wonderful, salty ambience, fine food, and an excellent staff. The kids will like the mounted river otter on display right across from the cashier. Lunches range from $6.00 to $15.00; dinners from $12.00 to $25.00. Open year-round. Call (843) 884–8102 or check out www .bigguynet.com.

Hurricane Hugo

After Hugo whipped through Charleston in 1989, it left a number of stories behind that seem to increase and get bigger every year. One is of the farmer who tied six chickens to six posts, hoping they wouldn't get blown away. The idea worked, and the chickens all lived to see another day—unfortunately the storm suction pulled out every single feather of every single bird. And the best line that's still around came from a mobile-home owner. "Man, when I looked outside in the morning there were refrigerators in the trees."

Patriot's Point Naval and Maritime Museum is in Charleston Harbor and is one of the most unusual and best-run museums in the country. A mile from the dramatic Arthur Ravenel Jr. Bridge over the Cooper River are four permanently moored ships, twenty aircraft, and the World War II aircraft carrier *Yorktown*. You will find the destroyer *Laffey,* the Coast Guard cutter *Ingham,* the submarine *Clamagore,* and the nuclear-powered ship *Savannah,* which can be boarded, inspected, and photographed at your convenience. Again, be sure to pack your camera and take along plenty of color film.

To give you some idea of the size and weight of the *Yorktown,* consider this: During Hurricane Hugo in 1989, which practically lifted Charleston up and set it back down again, the carrier barely moved. The ship served in combat at Truk, the Marianas, Iwo Jima, and Okinawa in World War II. Later it picked up the crew of *Apollo VIII,* the first manned spacecraft to circle the moon.

The hangar and flight decks of the carrier are now set up as a journey through the history of naval aviation. Here you'll see many of the prop-driven fighters, bombers, and torpedo planes that fought throughout the Pacific. You'll see a B-25 bomber similar to the ones of General Jimmy Doolittle's famous "Sixty Seconds Over Tokyo" raid. You'll see fighters that provided the air support during the Korean War. A great collection of some of the world's most feared jets is displayed here along with distinguished battle histories spanning from Korea to Desert Storm. You'll see the actual living quarters of the pilots and the "ready rooms" where they were briefed on their upcoming missions.

While aboard the carrier, you'll also want to stop by the ship's theater for a complimentary viewing of the 1944 Academy Award–winning film *The Fighting Lady,* which features some of the most incredible World War II dogfight footage ever taken.

The centerpieces on board the *Yorktown* are the twenty vintage aircraft ranging from a World War II basic trainer to the jets that ruled the skies of the Korean, Vietnam, and Persian Gulf Wars. They even have a World War II torpedo bomber much like the one former President George Herbert Walker Bush pancaked in the Pacific.

The museum is open daily from April 1 through September 30 from 9:00 a.m. to 7:30 p.m. From October 1 through March 31, hours are 9:00 a.m. to 6:30 p.m. Admission is $14.00 for adults, $7.00 for children ages six through eleven, free for children under six. Call (843) 884–2727. Visit www.patriotspoint.org.

If you're staying overnight in Charleston, the **Spiritline Dinner Cruise** is one of the musts on your list. Get on board the *Spirit of Carolina,* which leaves from Patriots Point in Mount Pleasant, for a three-hour evening of dinner, live entertainment, and the best possible view of the old city at dark. It's a beautiful trip and one you won't soon forget. The food, entertainment, and service are excellent. It gets cool out in the harbor, so take along a sweater.

Spiritline also offers a 1 1/2-hour sightseeing trip in the daytime and a 2¼-hour trip out to the Fort Sumter National Monument and Museum. Call for information at (843) 722–2628 or (800) 789–3678. Or you can go to www .spiritlinecruises.com.

Price for the dinner cruise Sunday through Thursday is about $40 per person. On Friday and Saturday, it's in the $45 range.

Prices for the Harbor Tour are $13.00 per person, $7.00 for children ages six to eleven, and free for children under five.

Prices for the Fort Sumter Tour are adults $13.00, children ages six to eleven $7.00, and children under six free.

Momma Brown's at 1471 Ben Sawyer Road, Mount Pleasant, is hard, hard, hard to beat. In the Carolina sweepstakes on barbecue, they're way out in front of the pack; no one else is even close. They specialize in the great vinegar-and-pepper–based sauce that is famous down here in the Low Country. Open Tuesday through Saturday from 11:00 a.m. to 8:00 p.m. and Sunday from 11:00 a.m. to 3:00 p.m.; closed Mondays. Prices vary from $5.00 to $7.95. Call (843) 849–8802.

Another amazing place, especially for eating South Carolina seafood, is ***Bowen's Island*** at 1870 Bowen's Island Road, Mount Pleasant. This unique restaurant is as rustic and back-roads as it can get. As a matter of fact, unless you're ready for it you'll take one look, hit reverse, and back right on out. But stick with it. First off, you have to find it. The best bet is to stop in the Folly Beach area and ask anyone. Everyone goes here and has been going here forever. Once you get over the shock of seeing it, you'll love it. Everything is fresh because for years the Bowens have been running the whole show— from procuring the seafood to cleaning it to getting it on the table. The dress code is ultra-casual, which means jeans are the top of the line. Inside the concrete-block house, which looks like a cell block, you'll see the old walls are covered with names and one-liners that go back to the 1940s. Check the spiral notebooks written in by generations of Bowen diners, and be sure to add your name and comments. Get here early and tour the holding tanks for the crabs and find out why Folly Beach oysters are the best on the coast. If you have any questions about crabs, oysters, clams, and seafood in general (such as how to tell when it's fresh or questionable or really off-limits), this is the place to find out the answers. The specialties here are fried shrimp, crab cakes, and all-you-can-eat oysters at prices you can't beat. Once again, don't be put off by the outside appearance; inside, once the food is served and the ancient jukebox is on, it's terrific. Open only Monday through Saturday from

friedoysters

It might not be on the menu, but you can ask for it and probably get it . . . fried oysters and yellow grits.

5:00 to 10:00 p.m. Prices range from $10 to $15 tops. No credit cards. Call (843) 795–2757.

At 819 Coleman Boulevard, Mount Pleasant, *J. Bistro* specializes in nouveau American, with a price range of $15 to $40 for dinner. Open Tuesday through Sunday 5:00 to 10:00 p.m. They also serve an excellent brunch on Sunday, from 10:30 a.m. to 2:30 p.m. Call (843) 971–7778. Or see www.jbistro.net.

Atlanticville Restaurant and Cafe, at 2063 Middle Street, Sullivan's Island, is located in a traditional island beach house, where you can sit on the patio before or after dinner and watch the sunset. Inside, the atmosphere is casual but the food is elegant, and there is an extensive wine list. One of the features here is Thai Tuesday, which is very popular with the natives.

Call (843) 883–9452. Open daily from 5:30 to 10:00 p.m. Sunday brunch from 10:00 a.m. to 2:30 p.m. Prices range from $5.00 to $10.00 for lunch and $25.00 to $35.00 for dinner. Their Web site is www.atlanticville.net.

Of course, no visit to Charleston would be complete without a trip to *The Battery.* But first a little background on the site. This tip of the Charleston peninsula was first called White Point Garden due to the white expanse of sand and the bleached oyster shells that identified it as a prominent marker when the colonists were settling here in 1670. The point later gained fame in 1718 when Stede Bonnet and nineteen of his fellow pirates "took the air" here with ropes around their necks, an event that brought an end to the coastal piracy that had plagued the nearby waters.

On April 12, 1861, Charlestonians sought vantage points here to watch the Confederate guns fire on the Union troops stationed at Fort Sumter. The cheers went up, Rhett Butler groaned (fictionally, years later in Margaret Mitchell's *Gone with the Wind*), and the Civil War had started. When Union

The Battery

Author's Note

One of the better walking-around stories down here about Charleston is about an elderly pair of sisters who had fallen on lean times. Despite their circumstances they insisted on telling everyone that nothing had changed and they were still summering in Paris. At night, when the rest of the town was asleep, they would slip out of their shuttered house and take their constitutional along The Battery. One night a child recognized them and wanted to say hello. Her mother held her back, saying, "No, dear, we don't speak to them in the summertime. They're still in Paris."

If this isn't the story that made Charleston "the most civilized town in the country," it certainly should be.

forces left Fort Sumter, the Confederates occupied it, digging in for the next two years under heavy bombardment and preventing the Union from taking Charleston.

In June of 1863, Union troops gained control of Folly Island and the mouth of the Stono River. On July 10 they crossed Lighthouse Inlet to the southern end of Morris Island and by nightfall had secured half of the island and were within artillery range of Fort Sumter, which by then had become a symbol of Confederate resistance. Defending the tip of Morris Island and Charleston at the place formerly known as White Point Garden was the Confederate Battery Wagner.

On July 18, the Union forces advanced up the beach. It was this battle that was depicted in the film *Glory*, starring Morgan Freeman, Matthew Broderick, and Denzel Washington. Spearheading the attack was the Fifty-fourth Massachusetts Regiment under the leadership of Colonel Robert G. Shaw, the twenty-five-year-old son of a wealthy Boston abolitionist. The bloody battle saw more than 40 percent of the black troops killed; Colonel Shaw died with them.

The courage of the Fifty-fourth proved once and for all to the leaders of the North and the South that black soldiers could fight. By 1865, a total of 178,895 black soldiers had enlisted in the Union Army—more than 12 percent of the North's fighting force. Recent southern historical work has shown that black soldiers also fought with the Confederacy.

By September the Union controlled all of Morris Island, only 1,300 yards of water away from Fort Sumter. For almost two more years, the Confederates held out under more heavy bombardment. Finally in February of 1865 they withdrew in the night when they knew Charleston city was falling to Sherman.

Today The Battery, filled with war memorials, cannons, and a monument on the spot where the pirate Stede Bonnet was hanged, is one of the most pleasant parks in the city and is the ideal place for turning the kids loose. You might follow the custom of hundreds of old Charlestonians who believe that no evening is complete without watching the sun set from here and then lighting up a cigar and taking a luxurious stroll along the ancient seawall.

Back in downtown Charleston, across from the visitor center is *The Charleston Museum* at 360 Meeting Street. Call (843) 722–2996 or visit www.charlestonmuseum.org. This is the first and oldest museum in the country, founded in 1773. Some exhibits focus on the Native Americans who were here first, others on the Revolutionary War or the Civil War; another celebrates the birth of the Charleston dance.

Children will especially enjoy the "Discover Me" room with amazing interactive exhibits. Toys, games, clothes, and even children's furniture have been collected from the past for entertainment and education. For a full grasp of old Charleston's culture and contributions to the country and to the world, no trip would be complete without a visit here.

Charleston has long prided itself on religious tolerance, evidenced by the fact that here you can find the oldest Baptist, Catholic, and Jewish houses of worship in the country.

The oldest of these is the *First Baptist Church* at 61 Church Street. Founded in 1682, the church was redesigned in 1820 by Robert Mills, the first American-born architect and the designer of the Washington Monument. This structure is one of the earliest Greek Revival buildings in the nation. Morning services and Sunday school are held here on Sunday; a vesper service is held on Sunday evening. Wednesday is Family Night, with supper and a prayer service. A concert series here features organ recitals and chamber music programs. Call (843) 722–3896 or see www.fbcharleston.org.

In 1839 *St. Mary's Church* was built at 89 Hasell Street. This is the oldest Roman Catholic church in South Carolina and is famous for its stained-glass windows, oil paintings, and graveyard. Call (843) 722-7696. Visit www.catholic-doc.org/saintmarys.

Kahal Kadosh Beth Elohim, at 90 Hasell Street, was founded in 1749 and is the oldest synagogue in continuous use in the United States. According to synagogue records, it is the oldest surviving Reform synagogue in the world. Services are held Friday evenings and Saturday mornings. Call (843) 723–1090 or go to www.kkbe.org.

St. Michael's Episcopal Church, on the corner of Meeting and Broad Streets near the Four Corners of Law at 14 St. Michael's Alley, was established in 1761. The simple and elegant structure with a walled graveyard has long

South Carolina's Jewish Tradition

Jews have lived in South Carolina for more than 300 years. The provisions for religious tolerance offered by Carolina's Fundamental Constitution were unique for the time, and news of the friendly environment spread across Europe and the West Indies. Most of Carolina's early Jews were people of Sephardic heritage whose ancestors had been expelled from Spain and Portugal centuries earlier. Over a hundred years before the Civil War, hundreds of Jewish immigrants came to South Carolina from Prussia and Poland. They were attracted to the Charleston area by the busy port, by the already established Jewish community and synagogues, and by the opening of the back country to settlers. Early settlers opened dry goods stores and became doctors, lawyers, journalists, and soldiers. Later they would fan out across North Carolina and into Georgia until every market town was served by at least one Jewish-owned shop. As time passed they ran the stores that were the very center of the community. They served the farmers who would come into town, buy things they needed, and run up accounts, which would be paid when crops came in.

In Charleston between 1905 and 1912, the Jewish population more than doubled. The neighborhood where they settled was called Little Jerusalem. At one time some forty stores on upper King Street were closed on Saturday, the Jewish Sabbath. The men held daily prayer services, the women kept kosher homes. They trained their African-American help to make potato kugel and gefilte fish, and they in turn were taught to fix fried chicken, corn bread, and okra gumbo.

Here is part of Isaac Harby's letter to Secretary of State James Monroe in 1816: "Jews are by no means to be considered as a religious sect, tolerated by the government: they constitute a portion of the People . . . Quakers and Catholics; Episcopalians and Presbyterians, Baptists and Jews, all constitute one great political family."

Rabbi Gustavus Pozanski, consecrating Kahal Kadosh Beth Elohim's new building in Charleston in 1841, said, "This synagogue is our temple, this city our Jerusalem, this happy land our Palestine."

And the last lines of Myer Moses' service before the Charleston Hebrew Orphan Society on October 15, 1906, may very well say it all: "Collect together thy long scattered people, and let their gathering place be in this land of milk and honey."

been a landmark and can be seen in many of the paintings and photographs of the old city. Call (843) 723–0603 or see www.stmichaelschurch.org.

Another beautiful church is *St. Philip's Episcopal,* 146 Church Street, on the corner of Church and Queen Streets. Both of these churches have been lovingly sketched and painted by Elizabeth O'Neill Verner; prints of these sketches are modestly priced and are available at the Gibbes Museum of Art gift shop, 135 Meeting Street. (See "Downtown Charleston," earlier in this chapter.)

Emanuel African Methodist Episcopal Church, 110 Calhoun Street, was organized in 1787. Its present building has been in use since 1891. With its congregation of more than 1,600 members, the church is very active in assisting the Charleston Interfaith Crisis Ministry as well as a score of charitable organizations. Two Sunday morning worship services are held here. A Thursday evening service and a Bible study group on Monday are also offered. Call (843) 722–2561.

A few years back I wrote a book entitled *Golfing in the Carolinas*. The assignment was simply to pick out the fifty courses in the Carolinas that I liked best, play each of them, write a few words, and then go on to the next one. I learned a great deal on my tour, especially about master architects Donald Ross, Alister McKenzie, Robert Trent Jones, Tom Fazio, and Pete Dye, whom I watched build the **Ocean Course** on Kiawah Island. This course, which hosted the 1991 Ryder Cup matches, is an absolute must for any golfer with a set of sticks. Incidentally, you go right by the Angel Oak on your way here (see "Gardens and Historic Plantations," earlier in this chapter).

Ten of the Ocean Course holes run right along the ocean. Considering the cost of oceanfront lots on Kiawah, the course may very well be one of the most expensive ever built. It is certainly the hardest to play. When the wind is up, which is almost every afternoon, very few golfers break 90. During the '91 Ryder Cup matches, pros were actually aiming into the gallery hoping to avoid the howling wind, and the pro Mark Calcavecchia was reduced to actual tears—he had to withdraw from the final holes. While windblown and terrifying, the Ocean Course is a course all golfers should play just to be able to say they tried it. Fortunately it's semiprivate, and a simple phone call to (843) 768–2121 or (800) 654–2924 can get you a tee time. Try to come early to avoid the afternoon wind, and bring plenty of balls. See www.kiawahisland.com.

golfcourses

While Charleston and the Low Country are only 5 to 10 feet above sea level, the land rises to 3,560 feet 200 miles away at Sassafras Mountain, west of Greenville. This elevation difference, along with the great varieties of trees and soil, accounts for the fact that South Carolina is considered by many to be the best state in the country for its variety of great golf courses.

While South Carolina doesn't have such venerable courses as Shinnecock out on Long Island, New York, or Brookline near Boston, it has something else—incredible golf weather. When you consider that northern courses are closed down four and five months a year and that down here in the so-called hard lard belt we play almost every day, the rest of the golfing country simply pales by comparison. South Carolina also has a wonderful variety of courses, ranging from the 4,000-foot mountain courses to the sandhills to the Low Country and the ocean. While most northern courses are private, most of South Carolina's are semiprivate, which means a great number of golfers will have the opportunity to play on a wide variety of great courses. A few of the better ones include Tom Fazio's famous **Harbor Course at Wild Dunes** on The Isle of Palms (843) 886–2164, (800) 845–8880, ext. 4, or www .wilddunes.com; Jack Nicklaus's Turtle Point on Kiawah Island; **Arthur Hill's Dunes West** in Mount Pleasant (843) 856–9000, (888) 955–1234, or www.golf duneswest.com; and Pete Dye's aforementioned Ocean Course on Kiawah. For more on all of Kiawah's golf courses, see www.kiawahresort.com.

Because Charleston offers so much to the visiting tourist, it may very well be the ideal city for the "golf widow" and the ever-growing number of "golf widowers." Cases are on file of golfers who arrive here determined to play four or five of the dozen famous courses around town but who, after looking at the calendar of events, the long list of great restaurants, and the sights to be seen, wind up not getting a single club out of their bags. But for the golfer who has to play, this is the place to do it. The truly spectacular courses here, which year in and year out make the list of the top fifty in the country, are the Ocean Course on Kiawah Island and at Wild Dunes on Isle of Palms.

For the golf historian, a trip out to the private **Charleston Country Club** should be fascinating. Despite the records showing that the first course in America was open for play in 1898 at St. Andrews in Yonkers, New York, the game was being played here almost 250 years earlier under the encouragement of King Charles II. King Charles was an avid golfer, and a 1698 print shows him being interrupted in the middle of a round to read news of an Irish rebellion. At the club you can see the old menus from the late seventeenth century and golf notices from the early eighteenth. For information, call the club secretary at (843) 406–0895.

Places to Stay in Charleston and the Surrounding Area

CHARLESTON

Ashley Inn Bed & Breakfast
210 Ashley Avenue
(843) 723–1848, (800) 581–6658
www.charleston-sc-inns.com

Charleston Riverview Hotel
170 Lockwood Drive
(843) 723–3000, (800) 968–3569
www.charlestonriverviewhotel.com

Francis Marion Hotel
387 King Street
(843) 722–0600, (877) 756–2121
www.francismarioncharleston.com

John Rutledge House Inn
116 Broad Street
(843) 723–7999, (800) 476–9741
www.charminginns.com

Maison Du Pre
317 East Bay Street
(843) 723–8691, (800) 844–INNS
www.maisondupre.com

Middleton Inn
4290 Ashley River Road
(843) 556–0500, (800) 543–4774
www.middletonplace.org/inn

MONCK'S CORNER

Rice Hope Plantation Inn Mepkin
Abbey Road
(843) 761–4832
www.ricehope.com

Places to Eat in Charleston and the Surrounding Area

CHARLESTON

Anson
12 Anson Street
(843) 577–0551
www.ansonrestaurant.com

Coast
39-D John Street
(843) 722–8838
www.coastbarandgrille.com

Marina Variety Store and Restaurant
City Marina
17 Lockwood Drive
(843) 723–6325

O'Reilly's Irish Pub & Seafood Tavern
288 King Street
(843) 577–0406
www.charlestoncrabhouse.com

Peninsula Grill
Planters Inn, 112 North Market Street
(843) 723–0700
www.peninsulagrill.com

WEST ASHLEY

Mustard Seed
1978 Maybank Highway
(843) 762–0072

MT. PLEASANT

R.B's Seafood Restaurant and Raw Bar
97 Church Street
(843) 881–0466
www.rbsseafood.com

The Southern Corner

Barrier Islands

South of Charleston and all the way to Savannah, Georgia, 100 miles away, the land stays only a few feet above sea level and has a border of sandy barrier islands. Tall cypress trees rise above the live oaks and long-leaf pines, and the rivers feeding into the inlets and the ocean are a dark tea color, owing to the tannic acid from the cypress and swamp roots. In the narrow strip of lowland along the coast is the subtropical growth in which are found such plants as the large palmetto, several dwarf palmettos, yucca, and evergreen holly. The grasses along the coast are panicum, water millet, and sea oats, all of which are necessary to sustain the life of the rolling dunes protecting the shoreline from wind and tidal erosion. The people along Route 17, working small truck farms and commuting to Charleston and Hilton Head for work, have changed very little in the last hundred years.

As you travel on Route 17, especially on the long section south of Charleston, you'll be traveling through a part of the South that has withstood much of the tides of change. For a deeper insight and appreciation you might read *Praying for*

N

0   15 mi
0   15 km

21

95

ALT 17

321

278

601

17

Edisto R.

Savannah R.

GULLAH COUNTRY

Edisto Island

95

21

Ridgeland

Burton

Beaufort

BARRIER ISLANDS

321

17

S. CAROLINA

GEORGIA

278

Fripp Island

95

278

Parris Island

ATLANTIC OCEAN

Hilton Head Island

17

HILTON HEAD

Sheetrock by Melissa Fay Greens. In a wonderful storytelling style, she tells of the old road and marvelously captures much of the African-American culture.

Before you begin a tour of the Edisto Island area, which is this chapter's first destination, here's a little history. In 1666 Robert Sandford's British expedition dropped anchor at Edisto Island and spent a pleasant week with the Edistow Indians. They were helpful, cordial, and friendly, and the delighted Sandford went back to London and spread the news that this was the ideal place for a British colony. While he was gone, the Edistows had second thoughts. When the settlers returned, the Edistows told them they had changed their minds about tourists settling among them and that the natives up in Kiawah country a few miles north were not only much friendlier but were actually looking for newcomers and would welcome them with open arms. The settlers got the message, weighed anchor, sailed back up the coast, and settled Charleston on the banks of the Ashley River.

In 1674 Edisto Island was purchased from the Indians by the Earl of Shaftsbury. Shortly after, Paul Grimball was granted 600 acres of land on the North Edisto River and built a plantation house. In 1686, Spanish marauders sacked the area and the plantation and destroyed the ***Grimball Plantation.*** Today, the remains of the foundation (made of tabby, which is a cement made of lime, sand or gravel, and crushed oyster shells) can still be seen near the river.

One hundred years before the British, the Spanish built a small mission here on the banks of St. Peire's Creek. Called Oristo, a variant on the Indian word *Edistow,* the mission was operated by members of the Jesuit Order. Today, only a single place name, Spanish Mount Point, recalls that period more than 300 years ago.

AUTHOR'S FAVORITE PLACES

African Village
Near Sheldon
(843) 846-8900
www.oyotunjiafricanvillage.org

Bay Street Trading Company
808 East Bay
Beaufort
(843) 524-2000
www.baystreettrading.com

Edisto Museum
8123 Chisholm Plantation Road
Edisto Island
(843)869-1954
www.edistomuseum.org

Red Piano Too
870 Sea Island Parkway
St. Helena
(843) 838-2241
www.redpianotoo.com

Rhett House
1009 Craven Street
Beaufort
(843) 524-9030
www.rhetthouseinn.com

Sheldon Church Ruins
Highway 21 and 235
Near Gardens Corner

Not far from the ruins of the Grimball Plantation at *Point of Pines* is an old graveyard of the early settlers. Unfortunately, the slate gravestones have worn smooth over the years and are barely legible, but if you look closely you can see some of the dates are before 1700.

The Edisto Island Historic Preservation Society runs *The Edisto Museum,* located at 8123 Chisolm Plantation Road. Each room is crowded with displays, books, old letters, and artifacts that trace the history of the island from the time of the Edistow Indians. One of the many attractions is an electronically controlled nature board on which you match animal prints to the animals. Kids love this; adults are baffled and generally give up fast. The museum is open only on Tuesday through Friday from 1:00 to 4:00 p.m. Admission is $3.00 for adults; $2.00 for students; free for children ten and younger. Private tours can be arranged by calling (843) 869–1954. Their Web site is www.edistomuseum.com.

Here on Edisto Island, you need to be aware that you share this rustic and historic real estate with more than a few alligators. If you see one, chances are there will be others nearby. *Note:* Keep kids and small dogs away from them. A fact no one seems to believe is that alligators have remarkable speed for 20 to 30 yards and have been known to do terrible damage to dogs, deer, children, and slow-witted adults.

alligatornews

If the approximate distance from the eyes to the tip of the nose is 8 inches, that means the gator is 8 feet long. Ten inches means 10 feet, and so on. And one more tip: They actually love marshmallows. If you feel you have to feed them, do it from the bridges. And one last tip—DON'T.

Another hazard down here in the Low Country is snakes! Keep the children away from creek banks, drain ditches, heavy leaf-covered areas, and woods. South Carolina has the distinction of having the biggest variety of poisonous snakes in the country. As a matter of fact, Beaufort County, a few miles south of Edisto, is the place where most of the snakes used for extracting venom for snakebite serum are captured. They are also gathered for carnival shows as well as for a sprinkling of Pentecostal churches that still practice snake handling, or "snake chunking."

None of the snakes will attack unprovoked, but if you step on one or scare one, that is a different story. Some of the coral snakes are especially lethal. Beautiful and tiny with exquisite red and yellow bands, they look like toys, but as the locals say, "they can kill you quicker than a train." This is an exaggeration, but an untreated bite can be very dangerous. How do you tell a lethal coral snake from nonlethal? Simple rule:

YELLOW ON BLACK, FRIENDLY JACK.

BLACK ON YELLOW, WILL KILL A FELLOW.

Hurricane and Tornado Facts

A hurricane test: If you hold up a sheet of plywood to a window and turn it loose and it sticks, hammer it in and head for a shelter.

A test to see if you're in a hurricane: Check the rain—when it hits your window it will flow up and not down. This is hard to believe until you see it. But if you do see it, it's too late.

During a hurricane, most fish and all shrimp go crazy and swim in circles, even leap in the air. Some of the smart ones, however, swallow rocks and sink to the bottom.

Birds fly low to the ground. Some get caught in the hurricane's eye and stay in it until the storm diminishes and thus wind up thousands of miles from home. Legend has it the snowy egret came from Africa in a hurricane eye.

During a hurricane dogs howl and run around in tight little dog circles. Horses get nervous and stamp the ground. Cats ignore it.

If you're in a mobile home, get out in a hurry.

If you're on the road, and you shouldn't be, don't stay in the car. Find the nearest concrete culvert and crawl, climb, or claw your way under and stay there.

If the eye comes over, keep in mind that the worst part may very well be on its way. This is especially true if you are in the 12-to-3 quadrant of the hurricane. Keep in mind the hurricane is spinning counterclockwise. This means the wind behind it—say it's at 30 miles an hour—pushes it 30 miles faster in the 12-to-3 quadrant and slows it down 30 miles in the 6-to-9. But don't take time to analyze this; get out of your car, stay out of mobile homes, and find that culvert.

The big killer in hurricanes down here is not the wind or the water but the locals who plug in home generators and forget to disconnect the outside line. What happens is someone will assume the line is dead and step on it or pick it up.

Another killer, almost as lethal, is chain saws. If you use one, make sure you don't under any conditions hold it above your head, and be absolutely certain your feet are planted firmly on something solid. You might also leave the beer in the car.

Tornadoes usually ride along on the edge of the hurricane and do tremendous damage. Since you won't be able to see them, there's no point in even watching for them. Just know they're out there and take every precaution.

For years churches were routinely destroyed during tornadoes, while the town saloons remained untouched. Finally a saloon keeper told a preacher to keep the church doors open the way he did. The preacher tried it and it worked. The word spread, and now churches and buildings of any kind leave their windows open when the storms threaten. So, wherever you're staying, crack your windows on each end when the storm warnings are announced.

Practical tip: Toss a few plastic gallon milk jugs (with tops) in your trunk. After a hurricane or a tornado they'll be worth their weight in gold for collecting and storing drinking water.

Speaking of snakes, a definite qualifier for "off the beaten path" status is the ***Edisto Island Serpentarium*** at 134 Highway 174. This is an indoor/outdoor museum facility dedicated exclusively to the recognition, preservation, and study of reptiles. Opened in 1999, the Serpentarium is the brainchild of two Edisto Island brothers, Ted and Heyward Clamp, and their more than 50 years of snake hunting in South Carolina and around the world. Here you'll find a wide variety of reptiles. Those not displayed indoors behind glass are viewed by visitors outdoors who look over low-walled enclosures to observe the snakes and other critters living in streams, climbing in trees, or basking on stumps or logs exactly as they would be seen if encountered in the wild. The hands-on staff is prepared to answer questions and demystify the understandable reluctance some may have for the subject matter. Admission is $10.95 for adults (thirteen and up), $8.95 for youngsters six to twelve, and $4.95 for children four to six. Check out their Web site at www.edistoserpentarium.com.

Edisto, they say, is not so much a place as it is a time—and a time, preservationists add, that has resisted change. The old plantation money was made from indigo and sea-island cotton. Since enormous labor was needed for planting, tending, and harvesting these crops, the island became a major entry point for slaves from Africa and Barbados. The landowners sought out and secured the most educated slaves, and because many came from African aristocracy, race relations here were much different than they were in the rest of the state. Incidentally, the single-room-wide house construction so typically found in Charleston is said to come directly from Barbados.

One of the oldest stories here is of the very young white girl Hepzibah Jenkins, who was raised by local slaves when her mother died and her father was imprisoned during the Revolution. Later she married the island's largest landowner. Years passed, and in 1810 Hepzibah decided she wanted to build the plantation slaves a Baptist church. This inflamed her husband and the result was their separation. But Hepzibah was undaunted and started baking bread in a tabby oven (constructed of sea shells, lime, and sand) at what became the Hepzibah Jenkins Bakery. She financed and built the first church in America founded by a woman. The old bakery eventually disintegrated and became overgrown with vegetation, but the church, which is still called the Baptist Church, can be seen on the left side of Highway 174 as you enter Edisto. At the back of the church is the ***grave of Hepzibah Jenkins,*** and over it her children have erected a monument that reads:

HER CHARACTER WAS SO STRONGLY CAST, AND HER IMPULSES WERE SO
GENEROUS, THAT SHE WAS AN OBJECT OF INDIFFERENCE TO NO ONE. THE
POOR AND THE AFFLICTED WERE SPECIAL OBJECTS OF HER CONSIDERATION.
BY THEM HER LOSS IS TRULY FELT, AND BY US WHO KNEW HER BEST, SHE
IS MOST LAMENTED.

Travel Tips

There is something truly sad about sitting in an air-conditioned car, biting into what you think is an egg or chicken salad sandwich, and tasting the damage done by three to five hours on the road. Take my advice—you really don't have to live like that.

One of my favorite sandwiches on the road is fresh egg or chicken salad with crisp bacon, lettuce, and mayonnaise on heavy-duty whole-wheat bread. But, and it's a big but, after an hour or so inside a wrapper, the bread picks up most of the moisture and breaks down. You might as well be eating tuna fish. I played golf in the Crosby Invitational a couple of years back, and Yogi Berra, of all people, showed me how they handle egg salad up in a place called the Bronx. You take the top slice of bread off and stack the egg or chicken salad with about an inch of thick cut potato chips. Then you place the top slice back on, and after taking a firm grip on everything, you're in business. Now you talk about a winner! This is it! If you don't believe me, try it at home before you start traveling. You'll never eat another soggy sandwich.

Another incident that illustrates the tenacity and independence of the Edisto people occurred in 1861. It was then, when South Carolina was debating whether to sign the Ordinance of Secession, that the Edisto Island delegate jumped to his feet and declared that irrespective of what the state did, Edisto Island would secede from the Union all by itself.

In 1810 vacationers from Charleston and Columbia began coming to the Edisto beaches. That same year Edingsville Island was developed by one of the island's wealthy cotton planters, William Edings. By 1820 he had built sixty large summer cottages and a boardwalk; the resort was comparable to Atlantic City, New Jersey, or Newport, Rhode Island. Photographs of ladies with hoop skirts and parasols and men in skimmers can be seen in the Edisto Museum. Unfortunately, the hurricane of 1890 destroyed everything standing, and the island returned to its formerly barren state as the barrier island it had been. It wasn't until 1994 that the first new house was built here. These days, only four homes are on the island. If splendid isolation (read: luxurious) sounds like your cup of tea, contact Vacation Rentals by Owner, listing #53342. Visit www.vrbo.com/53342.

Highway 174 dead-ends at Palmetto Drive. At the corner is ***The Pavilion*** restaurant, 102 Palmetto Boulevard, open for lunch and dinner six days a week, closed Tuesday. A good buy here (to share) is their steamed seafood pot, a medley of lobster tail, crab legs, oysters, clams, shrimp, corn, and sausage for $25. Beer and wine are served. Children are welcome and can be turned loose to walk along the beach. Call (843) 869–3061. Check out www.karma.com/biz/southcarolina/edistoisland/thepavilion.

Dave Lybrand owns and helps operate Edisto Realty, Inc. at 1405 Palmetto Drive. Call (800) 856–6538 for reservations for beachfront houses and villas and also creekside rentals. The variety of accommodations here is enormous. The Ocean Villa is rustic and right smack on the beach. The top floor has a huge porch overlooking the ocean where you can sunbathe, eat, drink, and be merry as you watch the long strings of pelicans gliding down the beach. I stayed here one year and counted eighty-six brown pelicans in one group. They often number more than a hundred. Private homes also are available for weekly rental. A beachfront house that sleeps eight averages $1,800 per week; houses off the beach range from about $600 to $1,200 in peak season. Visit www.edistorealty.com.

Coming into Edisto, you'll spot the **Old Post Office,** 1442 Highway 174, the premier restaurant on the island. The menu includes shrimp broiled with a mousseline sauce on whole-grained grits at $17 and a pecan-coated quail for the same price. A three-course dinner for two with wine should run you around $90. The coproprietor and chef, Philip Bardin, is a native here and can whip up the best Southern fare in the Low Country. The Old Post Office serves dinner only; reservations are required. Dress is casual. Closed Sunday. Open Monday through Saturday from May 1 through September and Tuesday through Saturday, October through April. Call (843) 869–2339.

Edisto Island, with more than 7 miles of uninterrupted beach, has managed to keep its landscape, skyline, and ecology about the way they were twenty or thirty years ago. It's still one of the real jewels on the South Carolina coastline. It's also one of the best areas in the entire country for collecting fossils. This is because this coastline was once a lengthy primordial bog, and today the tides and currents keep stirring it up. Sharks' teeth are easy to find, but they are nothing when compared to the fossils of some of the creatures that inhabited the area millions of years ago. Along these shores have been found the remains of elephants with tusks turned backwards, crocodiles 30 feet long, a 200-pound capybara (the biggest rodent in the world), birds with teeth and 19-foot wingspans, a ground sloth as big as a Volkswagen, horses with three toes, camels, tapirs, and saber-toothed tigers. Many vertebrate paleontologists still refer to the 1857 *Pliocene Fossils of South Carolina,* by Francis Holmes and Michael Tuomey, as the classic book about this science in the state.

Fairfield Ocean Ridge is a 350-acre resort with one-, two-, and three-bedroom villas for rent by the night or the week. Call (877) 296–6335. Golf packages can be arranged for playing the **Edisto Beach Country Club** (843–869–1111). The course is right on the property; many of the villas overlook the fairways. As a matter of fact, you can step out on the fairway with a nine iron and a bag of balls and get in all the practice you need. The greens fees and cart rentals are the lowest in the entire area, which is a notable fact since this is a 6,400-yard absolutely first-class course with wonderful greens and enough tight fairways to give any golfer all the challenge he or she needs. As a matter of cold fact, water comes into play on fourteen holes, and I'd suggest a long iron, rather than a wood, from many of the tees. The Tom Jackson–designed course is owned and operated by Jim and Patti Herrin, both golf enthusiasts, and they are doing a remarkable job keeping it in shape year-round.

Unlike most country clubs, where you have to know someone before you are allowed to pay—usually more than $100—to play, tee times here are unbelievably easy to arrange. All you have to do is show up at the pro shop with plenty of balls. In season greens fees are $50 before 2:00 p.m. and $43 after. For the golfer whose spouse doesn't play, this is probably the best course in the state where you can take him/her out for a lesson and have a great time doing it. Between the greens and tees are some wonderful walks through the live oaks, palmettos, and magnolia trees. Caution: When you walk near the lakes and creeks, keep your eyes peeled for the local alligators and an occasional snake. Armadillos, who have been spotted here recently, are harmless. This is also a wonderful spot for bird-watching; you're sure to see three or four great blue herons and all the brown pelicans you can count. If your spouse doesn't play, take him/her with you anyway for the cart ride through this really wonderful and unique area. The country club has an excellent restaurant between the ninth green and the tenth tee. One final suggestion: If you're planning on playing here, use the driving range at the other end of the island to warm up. For tee times or information, call (843) 869–1111 or visit edistobeachgolfclub.com.

At the north end of the beach is *Edisto Beach State Park.* Though small, the campground is one of the prettiest in the state. Many of the sites are set on small hills under live oaks and look out on the ocean only a few yards away. The campground is equipped with electrical and water hookups, barbecue pits, and a place to shower. A grocery store is only a block away. For those who love to camp or for folks on a budget, this is the ideal place to stay. While here you can explore the nature trails or go fishing, crabbing, or sailing. It is also an excellent place for bird-watching. For further information write Edisto Beach State Park, 8377 State Cabin Road, Edisto Island, 29438, or call (843) 869–4426.

For an elaborate rental house that is truly off the beaten path, call the Prudential Kapp/Lyons Agency at (843) 869–2516 or (800) 945–9667 and ask for information on Bucky Battle's house, *Whitmarsh,* at the end of Botany Road. The road is canopied by a beautiful tunnel of live oaks shrouded with Spanish moss. Visit www.kapplyons.com.

The house has six bedrooms and three-and-a-half baths; it can sleep as many as fourteen. The price is $2,095 per week in season, $1,695 off-season. The house, completely secluded and overlooking Frampton Inlet and the ocean, stands more than 40 feet high and, with its 180-degree view, has probably the best vista on the island. You can sit in the cocktail area at the top of the house and watch the leaping porpoises as they follow the shrimp boats into port in the afternoons. You will also see pelicans, egrets, herons, ospreys, ducks, geese, and even eagles. In the pastures off Botany Road, you can see egrets doing something rather strange. One egret will ride on a cow's back and pick off fleas, while two others high-step along in the grass eating the crickets and grasshoppers the cow flushes up. A little more bird lore here: Keep your eyes open—you may catch a glimpse of a Low Country painted bunting. This bird is a rare sight. With its blues, yellows, reds, and greens, it looks a great deal like a parrot straight out of the Amazon, only smaller.

You should also know that Edisto is a fishing paradise. You can fish here on the beach, from the creek banks, or from a john boat. John boats and surfing equipment can be rented for a nominal charge at **The Edisto Marina,** and you can fish almost anywhere you choose. They're at 3712 Dock Site Road, (843) 869–3504. Many local residents simply cast their lines from the bridges into the creeks or the inlets. Fishing here, you'll meet some of the resident characters of the island, and you'll get enough fishing advice to last a lifetime. One line you might hear from someone speaking Gullah is, "Most hook fish don' hep dry hominy," which means "The fish you almost caught doesn't do much for a plate of grits."

As you fish and watch the colors changing on the marsh grass and a long string of pelicans heading home right above you, you might consider what I. Jenkins Mikell, a plantation owner down here, once said: "Life here is one long dream. Here the art of being busy and doing nothing was brought to a fine point."

Leave Edisto on Highway 174, go to Route 17, and turn left to Gardens Corner, roughly 15 miles away back on the mainland. The land here remains about the same—low and sandy with pine trees, magnolia, and a dozen varieties of oak. Turn left on Route 21. Only 5 miles down the road is **Beaufort,** the second oldest town in the state, settled in 1711. During the Civil War the town was occupied by Union forces, which saved it from being burned. Today the big homes looking out over the inlet and the ocean are almost exactly as they were in 1860. You can get a very good idea of the look of the old town and its surroundings from any one of the following movies filmed here: *Glory, The Big Chill, The Great Santini, Forrest Gump, Conrack,* and *The Prince of Tides.* As a matter of fact, Pat Conroy (author of *The Prince of Tides*) spent his childhood here and later taught school down the coast out on Daufuskie Island. And as another matter of fact, the cast of *The Prince of Tides*—Barbra Streisand, Nick Nolte, and Jeroen Krabbé—all stayed downtown at Rhett House, one of the old mansions that have been converted to bed-and-breakfast inns. More on that later.

Your first stop should be the ***Visitor Information Center*** at 1006 Bay Street; the phone number is (843) 524-3163 and their Web site is www.beau fortsc.org. Here you can pick up a walking-tour map with points of particular interest marked out. They will also help you with suggestions for restaurants and places to stay if you are spending the night, which you should do. Mornings here on Bay Street, with its very large and very beautifully landscaped park that runs along the waterfront, are wonderful. The park backs up to restaurants, coffee shops, and the very well-run ***Bay Street Trading Company,*** 808 Bay Street, which not only sells current books and best-sellers but local books, local recipes, and the famous ghost books for which the area is known. They also have a good supply of my novels and short stories. They're at (843) 524-2000.

If you feel like walking a few miles, pick up a tour map and just follow the dotted lines. The map shows twenty-six historical sites, including ***St. Helena's Episcopal Church*** at 507 Newcastle Street, built in 1724, and the ***Beaufort Museum,*** located in the Arsenal (1798) at 713 Craven Street, a fascinating repository of the city's man-made history. There's more at www.historic-beaufort.org. If you're not too keen on walking, a much easier way of seeing the old town is from the seat of one of the very comfortable horse-drawn carriages that are parked at the curb and available at almost any hour. Prices run around $18 and the tour lasts about 50 minutes. If you are so inclined, take the ride right around sundown with an iced bottle of white wine.

At 1009 Craven Street is the aforementioned and internationally famous ***Rhett House.*** This bed-and-breakfast is the ideal place to stay in Beaufort, but you must make your reservations early. Actors, directors, and writers have been headquartering at this centerpiece long before *The Big Chill* was filmed in this area. The inn's hosts, Steve and Marianne Harrison, originally from New York, have a marvelous collection of candid photographs of Barbra Streisand, Nick Nolte, and Jeroen Krabbé all looking delighted with their accommodations and everything around them. Check the kitchen and ask the cook to show you the fascinating print that Jeroen Krabbé gave the Harrisons.

This old mansion, which is as ornamental as a wedding cake, has wraparound verandas, classic columns and porticos, and beautifully carved and finished entries and staircases. Fresh flowers are everywhere, and each and every appointment is in excellent taste. Every room has a small library; the main library has everything from Nabokov to Stephen King to Jackie Collins.

Rhett House

All guest rooms have televisions, telephones, and private baths; two have fireplaces. You can even sleep in the same bed that Barbra Streisand slept in. The management will be glad to arrange golf, tennis, swimming, and massages. Carriage tours, sunset cruises, and historic walks are also available. Rates are $195 to $325. Call (843) 524–9030 or visit www.rhetthouseinn.com.

Steve and Marianne are delightful and knowledgeable company and love to talk far into the night about books, the theater, and the movies. The excellent gourmet dinners here feature regional favorites such as crab cakes, fresh fish, roast lamb, and vegetables with herbs from the Rhett House gardens. You can even dine on the porch under the limbs of the great live oak in the front yard. On Sunday evenings the Harrisons offer elegant supper baskets as a dinner alternative. Room rates include not only wonderful accommodations but afternoon teas, bicycles, and a full breakfast. Smoking is limited to the porches, verandas, and garden. Ask about their seasonal "specials."

Two blocks from Rhett House at 906 Port Republic Street is a little gem of a restaurant called *Emily's.* Featuring a unique menu that includes twenty-nine different dishes called tapas, this is a spot that should not be overlooked. Just a few of the exotic dishes that represent the international flavor of the place are escargot Bourguignon, wild boar sausage, crabmeat Rangoon, and tempura shrimp. Emily's also has an excellent wine list. The bar at the end of the room is perfect for meeting a few of the more interesting local residents. Dress is casual. Open from 4:30 to 11:00 p.m. Monday through Saturday. Call (843) 522–1866 for reservations.

The *Two-Suns Inn* at 1705 Bay Street is a restored neoclassical Revival-style home that once served as a home for female teachers living and working here in Beaufort. Today it is a bed-and-breakfast and houses the weaving studio of innkeeper Carol Kay. Rates here are $150 per night and up. Call (843) 522–1122 or visit www.twosunsinn.com.

Four or five blocks away at 910 Bay Street is **Banana's,** which is about what it sounds like. The staff here call the place "the fun spot on the waterfront" and recommend you show up in shorts or jeans. Banana's serves hot dogs, homemade potato chips, eight different kinds of sandwiches, and nine kinds of half-pound burgers. If you're in the mood, you can order steak, ribs, or fresh shrimp. All meals are served with homemade bread. Prices range from $10 to $25. It's a great place to eat and linger and watch the locals watching the tourists and the tourists watching the locals. Open 11:00 a.m. to 10:00 p.m., seven days a week. The restaurant features live entertainment Thursday to Sunday. Call (843) 522–0910.

If you drive a few miles down Bay Street, you'll see the signs to **Parris Island;** follow them. Unlike most military bases, which discourage visitors, this active Marine Corps base welcomes them. Visitors may take a driving tour of the island; the tour leads through the old navy yard and to the site of the Spanish forts that were here in the seventeenth century. You can also visit the War Memorial Building on the base. Here you can see exhibits on the history and development of Parris Island and the history of the Marine Corps. The island is open year-round, Monday through Friday from 7:00 a.m. to 4:30 p.m. and on Saturday, Sunday, and holidays from 9:00 a.m. to 4:30 p.m. Call (843) 525–2951. For general information, visit www.mcrdpi.usmc.mil.

Leave Beaufort and head out over the Lady's Island Bridge for **Fripp Island,** about 25 miles away. The islands get confusing here—Lady's, Pritchards, Hunting, and then Fripp all stem off Route 21. Just follow the signs and you can't go wrong.

Gullah Country

Heading for the end of Fripp Island on Route 21, you'll pass through the tiny village of **St. Helena Island,** which is probably the center of the Gullah culture and language. These inhabitants of the South Carolina coast are the only group of African Americans who have been able to trace their roots to the villages of the Sierra Leone territory in West Africa. This heritage is evidenced most dramatically in the rice agriculture, cast-net fishing, and arts and crafts such as the coiled basketry of these lowlands, as well as the language and the music.

A half mile from the center of St. Helena Island is the **Penn Center Historic District.** This was the first school established in the South to educate the freed slaves. The center has sixteen buildings, including cottages for groups of up to one hundred, and a small museum dedicated to the language and culture of the blacks who were native to this region. Penn Center was designated a

National Historic Landmark in 1974. For additional information on the events that take place here, visit www.penncenter.com or call (843) 838–2432. Or, write to Penn Center Historic District, P.O. Box 126, St. Helena Island, SC 29920 The museum is open Monday through Saturday from 11:00 a.m. until 4:00 p.m. Admission is $2.00 for children and $4.00 for adults. On Route 21 in the middle of St. Helena Island, you'll find the *Red Piano Too,* Highway 21E. It's impossible to miss and is certainly the most interesting art gallery in the entire Southeast. The building, for years a big grocery store, is a high-ceilinged wooden structure that has been on the National Register for some years now and is a one-of-a-kind masterpiece. Red Piano Too exhibits and sells African-American artwork that ranges in price from $5.00 to $1,500.00. Much of the work is done locally, and the imagination and craftsmanship are truly remarkable.

One of the artists represented here is Everett Mayo, a former heavyweight boxing champion from Virginia. He was headed for a promising career when a construction accident left him legally blind in one eye. Everett then allowed his longtime love for art to emerge, and he began channeling his creative energies toward painted sculpture, Each piece of his work is done on driftwood found on the local riverbanks, and on this he paints his string of unforgettable animals, from wolves to tigers to a 6-foot-high giraffe and a 7-foot-long shark.

Red Piano Too also sells postcards, prints, Bibles written in Gullah, and small hand-painted memorabilia. The gallery even has a Pat Conroy Room where all of his books (autographed) are sold. If you are in Beaufort, or near Beaufort, or anywhere in South Carolina, this is a place you have to see. Call (843) 838–2241. Their address is 870 Sea Island Parkway, St. Helena, 29920. See more at www.redpianotwo.com.

Continuing on toward Fripp Island on Route 21, try *The Shrimp Shack,* 1929 Sea Island Parkway, which features casual family dining on an outside porch. Prices here are in anybody's ballpark. For about $8.50 you get a fried

Travel Tips

Here's a way to save money! Stop at the first rest stop in South Carolina and pick up a copy of the book of motel discount coupons. It's free. The lists are complete and come with detailed maps. In the current book some of the participating motels include Comfort Inn, Holiday Inn, Travelodge, Best Western, and so on. The motels and the rates may change from month to month, but the coupon book will spell this out for you as well as give you a good idea of exactly where to find the bargains. In the current book eighty-five motels are listed, along with their rates and general information. Don't forget this.

or boiled shrimp dinner with sides of red rice and coleslaw along with a Low Country hush puppy, which is a deep-fried corn stick shaped like a torpedo. The name goes back to the time when the kitchens to the plantations were in the backyards, and the cooks would toss corn bread to the yapping dogs and say, "Hush now, puppy." No reservations are necessary, but if you want to call ahead for a take-out order, call (843) 838–2962.

Gullah-n-Geechie Mahn Tours offers packages for bus tours as well as private van tours of the islands, where the Gullah culture is most apparent. You may choose tours that concentrate on such areas of interest as Gullah/ Low Country cuisine (Low Country boil or oyster roast); cultural performances featuring storytelling unique to the Gullah culture, dance performances, plantation melodies, blues, and jazz; and crafts and demonstrations that include sweet grass basket weaving, crabbing, shrimping, and net making. They will also make arrangements for your overnight accommodations, fishing, boat rides, and beach and shopping excursions, as well as golf and tennis games. Tour office hours are Monday through Friday 9:45 to 11:45 a.m., 1:45 to 3:45 p.m., and 4:30 to 6:30 p.m. Call (843) 838–7516 or (843) 838–6312, or write to P.O. Box 1248, St. Helena Island, 29920. Or, visit them at www.gullahngeechietours.net.

Still on Route 21 heading for Fripp Island, stop at *Gay Fish Incorporated,* 1948 Sea Island Parkway, for fresh shrimp and fish by the pound or the hundredweight. Charlie Gay also sells spices for cooking shrimp, cookbooks, and marine supplies. Eighteen boats dock at the pier here, and Charlie Gay says if you talk to any of the eighteen captains, you will be able to make arrangements to go out on a shrimp run. Call (843) 838–2763. If you want to go, set the alarm clock. The boats leave at 4:00 a.m.

Continue on Route 21 toward Fripp Island. This will take you to *Hunting Island State Park,* one of South Carolina's most spectacular parks. Located at one end of the park is the Hunting Island Lighthouse, the only one of the seven South Carolina lighthouses open to the public. The beach here is ideal for shelling. For an extraordinary view of the entire area, you can take a deep breath and climb the 181 steps to the top of the lighthouse.

Reservations can be made for rental cabins in the park. Write Hunting Island State Park, 2555 Sea Island Parkway, Hunting Island, 29920, or call (843) 838–2011. Their Web site is www.huntingisland.com.

While parts of this extraordinary, smooth beach are reserved for swimming and surfing, other areas are used by surf anglers. Comfort stations complete with showers are placed in several locations along the beach. The park also provides biking and nature trails. Open year-round from daybreak to dark.

As far as a lot of us down here in the Carolinas are concerned, the best and most accessible resort on the coast is *Fripp Island Resort.* Not only is

neattrivia

Near Yemassee there's a sign shaped like a hand with a long finger pointing to the message park yonder.

it remote enough to qualify as "off the beaten path," it has the perfect geography: a pristine beach on one side and a great sweep of tidal marshland on the other. Since tidal marshland cannot be developed, the resort will never get too big or too commercial or too anything. It's the perfect size. For an affordable resort Fripp has every amenity the larger resorts have but without the spread and the density and the impersonality that often comes with it.

For an idea of what the beach and the live oak and Spanish moss landscape looks like, pick up videos of two movies that were shot here: *Forrest Gump* and Disney's *The Jungle Book*.

When you rent a one-, two-, or three-bedroom condo or a beachfront house here, you automatically become a guest member of the Fripp Island Club and have full access to all of the resort facilities. Included in these are three top-notch golf courses. The latest, at Ocean Creek, was designed by Davis Love III and has been named one of the best new courses in the country by *Golf Magazine*.

In addition to the three courses, the resort provides a "Wee Links" setup on each course. This consists of tee placements for kids where they can play from shorter yardages and still be on a championship course. The advantage here is that your child can play along with you.

Fripp Island Resort, keeping the family in mind, has also provided a children's play pool with an alligator slide and giant frog and a lagoon-style pool with caves and waterfalls. Other facilities include croquet courts, a playground with a pirate ship, a basketball court, tennis facilities, and bike rentals. The tennis facilities are excellent, with eight soft courts and two hard courts. You can also rent skiffs, kayaks, or pontoon boats and take a trip on one of the beautiful creeks and waterways to watch for herons, ospreys, pelicans, and dolphins and explore the marshlands. Fishing tackle and crab and shrimp nets can be rented. Guided wildlife excursions are available for six passengers or fewer.

The food here at Fripp Island Resort ranges from excellent Low Country seafood and sizzling steaks served at the Ocean Grill Restaurant overlooking the ocean to hot dogs and ice cream at the sides of the three Olympic-size pools. Hugo's Cafe and Deli is famous for its pizza.

For the family that wants to live on or near the beach and wants to play golf or tennis, fish, crab, swim, and investigate the wildlife in a truly spectacular setting, Fripp Island Resort is where you should be.

Since the rates vary with the season and what kind of rental you are looking for, you should contact the resort for current rates. Write Fripp Island Resort, One Tarpon Boulevard, Fripp Island, 29920, or call (800) 845–4100. You can also visit www.frippislandresort.com.

Fripp Island Marina is located out on the end of Route 21 on Fripp Island at 28 Salt Wind Drive, St. Helena Island. Here you can fish from the 25-foot *Glory Halleluyah,* which can accommodate up to four guests. Captain Eddie supplies bait, tackle, ice, and all the instructions you need to make your trip first class. His Grady White–type boat is fully equipped with the latest electronics, head, icebox, stereo, and full cabin. He specializes in trolling for mackerel, kingfish, amberjack, bonito, barracuda, cobia, dolphin, wahoo, and sailfish. A full day is priced at $500, a three-quarter day is $400, and half a day is $300. If you haven't tried this, it's a real thrill. Just bring sunblock and wear soft-soled shoes. Call (843) 838–3782. For more on the marina events or navigational directions there, visit www.frippislandresort.com/marina.

From Fripp Island Marina go back through Beaufort on Route 21. As you leave Beaufort, the kids will enjoy stopping to climb upon and take pictures of the three jet fighters poised for flight at the gates of the Marine Corps Air Station.

Sheldon Church Ruins, on Route 21 near Gardens Corner, is something truly off the beaten path. It's a beautiful old brick Episcopal church set in the middle of three or four huge live oaks with a cemetery at the side and in the back with tombstones dating back before 1700. The old church has been burned three times and during the last 150 years has not even had a roof. But the simple brick columns still reach up and up into the Spanish moss, and the altar and front facade, highlighted with the sun streaming through the leaves, give it a grace and dignity that require nothing else. Sunrise services are held here every Easter morning; if you're within 100 miles, drive over—it will be an experience you will never forget.

Farther out Route 21, just before you hit Interstate 95, are two spots the kids will like. The first is **Pocotaligo,** which is the smallest town in the state. As reported earlier, the name is a short version of "poke a turtle's tail and he will go." The town is so small it has only one sign and the last population count was fewer than twelve. Natives joke that it's more of a place than a town. Tourists coming through often stop and back up to take a photograph of the sign.

Nearby is **Hobo Joe's,** which is next door to **Sad Sam's,** which is across the road from **Jolly Joe's.** Together, all three of these places look like a series of sideshows at a carnival. But they're not. This is the way we merchandise fireworks down here in the "hard lard belt." At any one of these places, you can buy anything from penny firecrackers to bottle rockets to $50 ten-stage Roman candles that go as high as 500 feet. You can even buy $100 extravaganzas that fire one hundred salvos and end with a Fourth of July celebration that looks not unlike the New York City fireworks on the East River. This will be a great treat for the kids because South Carolina law allows you to take them out in any uninhabited field and fire away. Everybody does it. So get plenty of punk for lighting your explosives and have fun. Caution: Be sure to use long sticks of punk to light fireworks and make sure the fuse is sticking straight out. And don't hold exploding Roman candles.

Hilton Head

The resident Indians here on Hilton Head fought off the settlements of the Spanish, the French, and the British until the middle of the 1700s. At that time they finally were overwhelmed by the British, who took over the area, introduced indigo, cotton, and rice, and started what was to become a boom economy that lasted until after the Civil War. Much hand labor was used to turn the leaves of the indigo plant in the cakes of blue dye that were in great demand at this time all around the world. Part of that labor involved stirring the steaming vats of foul-smelling indigo with long paddles. Slaves were imported from Barbados and later from Africa to accomplish this task and many others. When the slaves were freed after the Civil War, the planters left the island to them and went back to Charleston and inland to the Upcountry of South Carolina. The freed slaves now owned and worked the land and developed the Gullah culture with its own language, which is a mix of English, African dialects, and Calypso-sounding French. It is wonderful to listen to once you get the hang and rhythm of it.

In the twentieth century the island's climate and beautiful beaches began attracting developers who began buying land on the island. Slowly but inexorably, the blacks with their rich Gullah tradition were forced to leave the land. Many of them work today in service jobs on Hilton Head Island, and a few own small businesses there, but many have moved to the mainland around Bluffton. Luckily much of the Gullah tradition is still present here and can be seen in the Low Country cuisine, arts, music, and language.

Today Hilton Head has much to offer the tourist. The main attractions are the greatest concentration of outstanding golf courses, tennis facilities, fishing marinas, and accommodations in the country. All twenty-five golf courses are on the big island and neighboring Daufuskie Island. A few courses are private and thus for members only, but most are available for guests of the hotels and villas.

The winters are very mild here, but the ocean water is still very cold. You can't go swimming in the ocean, unless you do it for a very few seconds, but you can play golf and tennis, ride bikes, take a nature walks, and go sailing and deep sea fishing.

The MCI Heritage Golf Tournament in mid-April is internationally famous and is played on the weekend after the Masters Tournament in Augusta, Georgia, right across the South Carolina border. Tickets for the Heritage are usually available, and it is one of those rare tournaments where you can actually walk right along the course with your favorite professional.

Palmetto Dunes is perhaps the ideal spot on Hilton Head to bring a sports-minded family. This 2,000-acre resort has three championship golf courses, the nationally acclaimed Rod Laver Tennis Center, a deep-water marina, and more than three miles of uninterrupted beach. Uninterrupted here means that sometimes you won't see a single soul for a mile. For reservations and information call (843) 785–1138 or visit their Web site at www.palmettodunes.com.

While there is such a thing as a Palmetto Dunes Club private membership, and the feeling is definitely that of a private club, all three courses here and the tennis courts are open year-round to the public. Guests at the Hyatt Hotel and the Mariner's Inn here at Palmetto Dunes are given preferential tee times and reduced rates. Incidentally, these are the golf courses former President Clinton played every spring when he came to the island for the Renaissance Convention.

Roadside Religion

A sign near Sheldon painted on a 4' x 8' piece of plywood beckons visitors to venture down "Safari Road" to visit the African Village founded in 1970 by King Oba Ofuntola Adelabu Adefunmi. The king, who has been on Oprah defending his right to practice polygamy, is a former used car dealer who was smart enough to see the tax benefits of starting not only his own religion ("New World Yoruba") but also his own country. Oyotunji is not part of the United States.

I have been here three times now, and each time I get a different version of what the king and his followers are doing. At one time they were living exclusively off the land in preparation for returning to Yoruba, their ancestral home. Recently they have been trying to attract the tourist trade, and today they offer guided tours of their village and their way of life. The last time I was here my guide was wearing a colorful dashiki and proudly showed me his decorative facial scars. He spoke in a rapid-fire singsong with many Yoruba words and glottal clicks thrown in and was worth the modest admission. Unfortunately, the "Royal Palace" where the king and his many wives reside looks as if it has seen better days. But if you're within 50 miles, you should go here and listen to the drums and hear the pronouncements. It's harmless and safe and a place you'll never forget. You can also buy curious handmade mantelpiece items at rock-bottom prices. No phone. No pool. No pets.

While the Hyatt and the Mariner's Inn are stunning places to stay, many prefer the more informal villas, which are ideal for families. The villas as a group are like a giant two-story hotel spread around twenty-five pools; the result is that every three or four villas have semiprivate swimming.

You can rent a two- or three-bedroom villa facing the tennis courts, one of the golf courses, or the ocean. You can even rent one on a stream with a free canoe tossed in. If you have enough scout merit badges, you can pack your golf clubs or tennis racket carefully in the middle of the canoe and paddle to the course or the court. The villas come equipped with wonderful kitchens; supermarket shopping is less than a mile away. If you're traveling with children, you can use the babysitting and day-care facilities here, and if the kids are turned loose on the ocean or at one of the pools, there are plenty of well-trained lifeguards. The villas offer a unique combination of privacy and convenience to the golf courses, tennis courts, supermarkets, and a mall of outlet stores.

celebritynews

Watch for a sign near Bluffton:
WELCOME TO BLUFFTON, S.C., HOME OF
JOE FRAZIER.

While Hilton Head may appear to be crowded in the high season—spring and fall—Palmetto Dunes is set way back from the main road, and the traffic is completely off the beaten path. As a result, the resort offers as much isolation as you want.

Alligators up to 14 feet long thrive among the creeks and lakes here at Palmetto Dunes, as do raccoons, deer, and an occasional red fox. In the evening, possums pad from one house to the next looking for handouts. If you stand still long enough at night, there's a good chance of seeing one of the four or five native owls. Bird-watching here is like no place in the country. Audubon Society members, who come here often, have recorded more than 120 species in the immediate area. Watch for the painted bunting, the indigo bunting, the osprey, and the black skimmer, who glides along flashing its red bill to attract the fish, then makes a 180-degree turn and comes back and scoops them up with the lower part of its bill. The bird only operates when the water is calm. But watch for them, they're out there.

Harbour Town, located around the rim of Calibogue Sound, is dominated by the candy-striped *Hilton Head Lighthouse.* The cove, with its ninety-odd-slip yacht basin, is home for the serious boaters who travel the Intracoastal Waterway. A pleasant pastime here is to sit on one of the many rocking chairs with a drink or an ice cream cone or nothing and watch the boats coming in as the sun sets. If you've watched the Heritage Classic Golf Tournament on television, this area will look familiar. Surrounding the cove is a series of upscale shops, restaurants, and condominiums.

Directly across from the cove is the **Heritage Grill,** located in the clubhouse of the Harbour Town Golf Links. This small grill looks out over the ninth hole of the course and the putting green. The grill is open daily for breakfast and lunch. Dinner is offered Wednesday through Sunday. Call (843) 363–4080 for reservations.

Also near the lighthouse in Harbour Town is the fashionable **Cafe Europa,** at 160 Lighthouse Road, which is open for breakfast from 9:00 to 11:00 a.m. Monday through Friday, 9:00 a.m. to noon on weekends, for lunch from 11:00 a.m. to 2:30 p.m. daily, and for dinner from 5:30 to 10:00 p.m. daily. Call (843) 671–3399. Their Web site is www.cafeeuropahhi.com.

Ron Cerudo and Doug Weaver, two of the best pros that ever played on the PGA Tour, are now in residence at **Shipyard Plantation** (843–290–6726), where they give group lessons. Both Ron and Doug have won some of the biggest tournaments in the country. Today they are rated with the best of the best as instructors of the game. Both feel that amateurs' main problems stem from their setup, grip, and stance, and they believe every lesson should begin by working on these basics.

They are both excellent in short-game management and believe the basic chip and run should be a great deal like the putting stroke. They also believe in changing amateurs' basic swing as little as possible and trying to get them to believe in tempo and balance.

Rates are $80 for 45 minutes; kids twelve and under, $50. For more on Hilton Head Island golf, go to www.hhisleinfo.com and click on "golf."

Back Roads You Don't Want to Be Out on Too Late at Night

Route 275 out of Harleyville is a two-lane blacktop winding through a part of the old Palmetto State that may never change IMPEACH EARL WARREN has faded badly on the smooth rocks and runoff culverts, but GET US OUT OF THE UN is still with us in fresh spray paint, along with directions for where to buy night crawlers, crickets, and she-crab soup, and where you can get a good head, palm, or root reading. One sign in tortured hand lettering outside Bluffton—the area that gave the world Father Devine, Reverend Ike, Joe Frazier, and recently Del Webb—looks as if it has been lifted from The Guinness Book of World Records: MAN HAS GOTTEN AWAY WITH MORE SIN AND UNRIGHTEOUSNESS DURING THE PAST TWENTY YEARS THAN DURING ANY PERIOD SINCE GOD DROVE ADAM AND EVE FROM THE GARDEN OF EDEN.

Back on U.S. Highway 278 at the Gateway to Hilton Head is the *Low Country Factory Outlet Village,* 1414 Fording, Bluffton. This mall, with more than forty name-brand merchants, is the area's largest outlet shopping center. Some of the brands are Eddie Bauer, J. Crew, and Polo. Call (843) 837–4339. A full list of the outlet stores is at www.explorehiltonhead.com.

When you tire of golf and shopping, head for *Reilly's Grill and Bar,* 7D Greenwood Drive, Hilton Head Plaza. Call (843) 842–4414. Very popular for lunch and dinner, it's a combination grill, bar, sports bar, and hangout. Several televisions are always honed in on whatever sports event is in the air. Hamburgers and fries are especially good here, as are the coffee and desserts. The average lunch will cost you about $8.00; you can spend more for dinner, but try the burger first. The waitresses are friendly and funny. This is a great place to have a beer and watch the local action. There's a very good chance you'll come back. Open seven days a week from 11:00 a.m. to 11:30 p.m.

A few words about alligators on Hilton Head and all over the Low Country. I played golf here with a comic named Kenny Davis who had never been north of Tahoe or east of Vegas. He had never been to a zoo, and the only alligators he had ever seen were in the movies. I told him I could guarantee that he would see at least a dozen when we played golf on Hilton Head.

Well, we teed off, and perhaps the cloud cover was too thick or too thin or the pollen count was wrong, but for some reason we didn't see a single gator—only egrets, pelicans, doves, and an occasional pileated woodpecker. Finally, on the seventeenth hole, long after Kenny had decided that there was no such thing as an alligator, there beside a lagoon lay a monster that looked longer than my Ford.

Kenny looked at it and began laughing. It was so big and looked so ridiculous and so asleep, he thought it was something plastic up from Disney World that I'd had some redneck buddy blow up for his benefit. Before I could stop him, he was prodding the beast with his putter. And then two strange events happened simultaneously. The alligator's mouth opened, and the monster rose up in a hissing, rushing lunge. Kenny did a quickstep and levitated 2 or 3 feet, straight up. He did some aerial acrobatics, hit the ground running, and didn't turn around until he was 100 yards down the fairway. He was no longer laughing. Yes, Virginia, there are alligators down here.

Places to Stay in the Southern Corner

BEAUFORT

Beaufort Inn
809 Port Republic Street
(843) 521–9000
www.beaufortinn.com

Craven Street Inn
1103 Craven Street
(843) 522–1668
www.thecravenstreetinn
.com

Cuthbert House Inn
1203 Bay Street
(843) 521–1315
www.cuthberthouseinn
.com

The Old Point Inn
212 New Street
(843) 524–3177
www.theoldpointinn.com

Places to Eat in the Southern Corner

BEAUFORT

Rhett House Inn & Fine Dining
1009 Craven Street
(843) 524–9030
www.rhetthouseinn.com

EDISTO ISLAND

Old Post Office Restaurant
1442 Highway 174
(843) 869–2339

Pavilion Restaurant
102 Palmetto Boulevard
(843) 869–3061

RIDGELAND

Plantation Inn Restaurant
Highway 17
(843) 726–5510

ST. HELENA ISLAND

Shrimp Shack
1925 Sea Island Parkway
(843) 838–2962

TO LEARN MORE ABOUT THE SOUTHERN CORNER

Greater Beaufort Chamber of Commerce
1106 Carteret Street
Beaufort 29902
(912) 644–6400
www.beaufortsc.org

The Grand Strand

Fishing Villages and Wildlife Refuges

Along the coastline north of Charleston, the land stays about the same as in the preceding areas for about 100 miles: sandy beaches, barrier islands, and thick swampland. Then around Surfside and northward the islands begin to thin out and a great wide beach, known as the Grand Strand, takes over and continues all the way to the North Carolina line.

Forty miles north of Charleston on Route 17, the tiny village of McClellanville has sat peacefully under the live oaks along Jeremy Creek for the past 200 years. This quaint little commercial fishing village came into national prominence in late September of 1989 when the full brunt of Hurricane Hugo hit here and destroyed or damaged every standing structure. At the height of the storm most of the citizens of McClellanville, who thought they were safe inside the brand-new Lincoln High School, were playing cards by flashlight, listening to their radios, and sleeping. Suddenly the storm punched out thirteen air-conditioner casements, and water cascaded down the halls and into the rooms. Inside the cafeteria/auditorium

THE GRAND STRAND

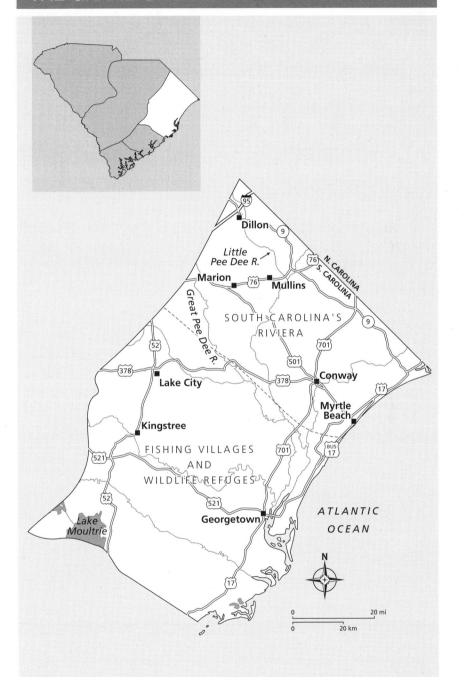

Dillon

95

9

Little
Pee Dee R.

76
N. CAROLINA
S. CAROLINA

Marion

76

Mullins

SOUTH CAROLINA'S
RIVIERA

9

Great Pee Dee R.

52

701

501

378

378

Conway

17

378

US 378

Lake City

Myrtle
Beach

Kingstree

FISHING VILLAGES
AND
WILDLIFE REFUGES

701

BUS
17

521

521

Georgetown

ATLANTIC
OCEAN

52

Lake
Moultrie

17

N

0   20 mi
0   20 km

where 1,200 people were gathered, the water quickly reached the incredible height of 6 feet, 1 inch. To save themselves from drowning, the men, women, and children climbed up on desks, tables, and chairs and the small stage at the end of the big room. Many men and women, standing on chairs standing on tables, punched out ceiling panels and placed their children up on the thin metal support beams, where they stayed until the storm finally stopped around 3:00 in the morning.

One teacher in charge of a group of infants and some elderly people on the far side of the building thought she would spend the night high and dry in her small classroom. But when she looked outside through the glass-partitioned steel door, she almost had a heart attack. Before her very eyes, shrimp and fish were swimming by. The water outside the building had risen to more than 10 feet. Quickly she led her charges down the dark halls to the cafeteria only to face the unbelievable sight of the fast-rising water. Miraculously the water stopped rising at 6 feet, 1 inch. Even more miraculously, no one was injured.

It took McClellanville more than five years to rebuild, but the marks that Hugo left behind will be here forever. At the Lincoln High School, a bronze plaque at the entrance to the cafeteria shows where the water crested.

McClellanville only has one bed-and-breakfast—***The Village Bed and Breakfast,*** 333 Mercantile Road, owned and operated by Cheri and Matthew George. This very quaint one-room unit is attached to the main house by a breezeway. During Hugo the entire place floated completely off its foundation,

AUTHOR'S FAVORITE PLACES

Brookgreen Gardens
Route 17 at Murrells Inlet
1931 Brookgreen Drive
Murrels Inlet
(843) 235–6000
www.brookgreen.org

Georgetown Ice Company
Georgetown
300 North Fraser Street
Georgetown
(843) 546–6169

House of Blues
4640 Highway 17 South
North Myrtle Beach
(843) 272–3000

Tidewater Golf Club
1400 Tidewater Road
Myrtle Beach
(843) 249–3829
www.tidewatergolf.com

Yawkey Wildlife Center
Route 17 near Georgetown
c/o SC Dept. of Natural Resources
(803) 734–3886
www.dnr.sc.gov/managed/heritge/
tomyawkey/description.

but the Georges had it hauled back and everything was repaired. Matthew, along with being a first-class carpenter, is an artist who works in oils, watercolors, and prints. Much of his work is on display here and is modestly priced. Call ahead for reservations or for a look at his artwork. Call (843) 887–3266.

If you would like to see **Lincoln High School** and the high-water mark in bronze in the cafeteria, and maybe hear some more Hugo stories, turn left on Dupre to Lincoln Road. The school will be right in front of you. Most of the school's current faculty was here the night Hugo struck; everyone has a fascinating story.

The **McClellanville United Methodist Church** on the corner of Pinckney and Dupre is ideal for a photograph if you step back far enough and get a shot through the live oaks when the sun and shadows are right. Another block away is the brown-shingled **St. James Episcopal Church,** which is also surrounded by live oaks. The last time I was here at least a dozen mockingbirds were up in the trees. If you're from anywhere north of Yonkers and have trouble identifying mockingbirds, just look for the sergeant's stripes on their wings. You can also whistle a three-, four-, or five-note tune and, if you're lucky and they're in the right mood, they'll play it back for you.

Nearby is the tiny village of **Awendaw,** which was also leveled by Hugo. Oysters from here and nearby **Bull Bay** are famous all over South Carolina. The village owes much of its livelihood to their preparation for shipping.

Sewee Bay, a mile or so away, was named for an Indian tribe, and on its shores are numerous mounds of refuse and broken pottery from their prehistoric dwellings. After the white settlers came, the Sewee Indians felt that the English were not giving them a fair deal, so they planned to seek the English king and personally lay their grievances before him. Building huge canoes, they sailed into the open sea and were never heard from again. A pirate captured soon after the Indians' disappearance swore that he had seen the canoes far out in the Atlantic.

Not to be confused with the Sewee war party that struck out for England, the **Sewee Restaurant,** back down the road on Route 17, is probably the finest spot on the coastline for fresh seafood. Check them out at www.coastal-sc .com/crabpot. The phone number is (843) 928–3609, and the hours are from 11:00 a.m. to 9:00 p.m. Monday through Thursday, 11:00 a.m. to 10:00 p.m. Friday, 8:00 a.m. to 10:00 p.m. Saturday, and 11:00 a.m. to 3:00 p.m. Sunday. Prices for lunch start at $8.95 and go up to $18.95. The delicious dinners range from $8.95 to $19.95. Because Sewee is only a few miles from McClellanville, they get all of their shrimp, soft-shell crabs, and flounder right off the boat. In other words, this is fresh seafood that really means fresh. You might even enjoy going to the McClellanville docks, watching the boats come in, and then taking the pleasant ride back through the old fishing town that Hugo almost destroyed but is now back up to speed.

Still on Route 17, a couple hundred yards south of the McClellanville turnoff, you can stop at the ***Crab Pot,*** 10024 Highway 17, for a very fine lunch or dinner. This airy, friendly spot right on the highway serves an excellent shrimp salad as well as hamburgers for lunch and a full menu for dinner. Prices range from $5.00 to $8.00 for lunch and up to $14.00 for dinner. Call (843) 887–3156.

Close by on Route 17—you'll have to watch for the signs—is *Hampton Plantation.* Set back from the road on a 2.5-mile drive, this is one of the finest examples of antebellum architecture in the entire South. When Henry Middleton Rutledge departed Hampton to serve the Confederacy during the Civil War, he left behind one of the grandest homes and most prosperous agricultural enterprises in America. The decades before the Civil War witnessed the high point of rice cultivation in South Carolina, and Hampton Plantation was one of the leaders. At this time Hampton was using the daily action of the tides on the freshwater rivers to irrigate the fields.

When Colonel Rutledge returned to Hampton Plantation in 1865, he returned to an entirely different South, one in which Hampton Plantation would never again hold the position it once had as a center of political and economic life in the state. The grand house remained unpainted and in decay; cotton was stored in the grand ballroom; crops were planted among the live oaks on the once stately lawn. By 1923 both the colonel and his wife were dead, and the house stood abandoned.

The colonel's son, Archibald Hamilton Rutledge—outdoorsman, writer, and the first poet laureate of South Carolina—returned to Hampton from teaching school in Pennsylvania and at age fifty-six began a long process of renovating the mansion. He described his labor of love in his best-known book, *Home by the River:* "When I first came back, it was sagging in places and it had not been painted in a generation. Now everything has been done to restore it without changing it and it gleams under its four coats of white paint. It is no unusual thing for visitors to tell me that in its simple dignity it is the most impressive home they have ever seen."

Now protected under the auspices of ***Hampton Plantation State Park,*** 1950 Rutledge Road, the mansion may be opened by appointment or rented for special occasions. A nominal fee ($4.00) is charged for admission to the mansion. A guided tour of the house, the grounds, and the nature trails surrounding the mansion can be arranged by calling (843) 546–9361. The park itself is open daily year-round from 9:00 a.m. to 6:00 p.m. The mansion is open year-round Thursday to Monday from 1:00 to 4:00 p.m. It is closed Tuesday and Wednesday. There is also a tour boat that carries you out to nearby Bull Island. Times and fares are available on request. Of the several related Web sites, I think the best is www.south-carolina-plantations.com/charleston/hampton .html. You can also visit www.southcarolinaparks.com.

While this plantation is truly one of the great sights of this part of the country, the unsuspecting traveler must be warned of a little item down here that can cause considerable discomfort—the deer fly. This noxious little beast can reduce a full-grown man or woman to quivering suet in minutes. Be prepared by picking up an insect repellent from Buster Brown back in McClellanville. Long-sleeved shirts are also advised. Travel tip: The deer fly is not confined to the Hampton Estates—it is literally everywhere down here. Also abundant are the no-see-ums and gnats. In any case, insect repellent and long-sleeved shirts will solve what could be a terrible problem.

A friend of mine interviewed a 110-year-old gentleman not too long ago and posed the question of what was the most important single invention he had witnessed in the century behind him. The old man counted on his fingers: the automobile, the airplane, the atomic bomb, landing on the moon, and the computer. Then he said, "Now these are all very fine, but you know something, if I've got to go with the one that's the most important for me, I've got to go with screens."

On up Route 17, a mile and a half north of Georgetown, turn off at the sign for **Hobcaw Barony** and go to the **Kimbel Lodge** at the right of the gate, at 22 Hobcaw Road. At this wildlife refuge you can collect enough wildlife information to last a lifetime. A sample of the free seminars is "South Carolina Butterflies and How to Attract Them" and "Voices of Spring: What's Happening to Our Migratory Songbirds?"

Wildlife trips include "The Interesting World of Oysters." The course blurb reads, "Live marine critters will be collected and viewed with microscopes at the Baruch Marine Lab. Participants will also learn how to safely harvest these razor-sharp bivalves. We'll even steam some for those who still have an appetite for oysters after studying the creatures that live in and around them. Wear old clothes and bring gloves and boots for walking in the mud."

This four-hour tour is limited to twenty people; the fee is $20. Other tours originating from Kimbel Lodge are "The Fishes of North Inlet Estuary," "Songbird Banding Workshop," and "Birds of Punkinseed Island." Learn more at www.hobcawbarony.org. or call (843) 546–4623.

The modern history of Hobcaw Barony began at the turn of the century. In the winter of 1905, Bernard Baruch acquired all of the land that once made up ten rice plantations. Hobcaw's tranquil woods and waters provided Baruch with recreation and relief from the pressures of public life. Baruch shared the peaceful world of Hobcaw with his family, friends, and many distinguished associates, including Sir Winston Churchill and President Franklin Delano Roosevelt. In the old mansion you can see photographs of Baruch on various hunting trips as well as shots of him with Churchill and Roosevelt. The barony includes about 9,000 acres of tidal wetlands, oyster reefs, former rice fields, and waterways on or bordering the Belle W. Baruch Foundation's 17,500-acre wildlife refuge.

The Kimbel Lodge at the entrance to the estate has wonderful exhibits of Low Country animals and plants. The kids will be especially delighted with the live baby alligator, but for goodness' sake, don't touch it! Check out their latest programs at www.hobcawbarony.org. Or call (843) 546–4623.

If you're hungry and heading north on Route 17, watch on the left side of the road for the sign for **_Hog Heaven._** There's no address here, but if you miss it you can make a U-turn and go back. The old owner, George Young, used to say, "Some people on the road smell the smoke and make the turn and come back." Hog Heaven, formerly Yum's Barbeque, has the finest pork

On Barbecue

When you arrive in the Palmetto State, you are in the official Tigris and Euphrates land of barbecue. Right down in here is where it all began. You have probably heard how Texas claims they have the best. Well, we shall now put that myth to rest. The Lone Star State, while it may have many wonderful things, does not have hickory wood. Without hickory wood you cannot have true barbecue. Now they may call what they serve barbecue, because it's a free country and they can call anything they cook, serve, and eat anything they want. But around here, if you mention Texas barbecue someone's going to drift out to the parking lot and check your license plates.

Down here in the "hard lard belt," our barbecue is cooked with hickory wood and hickory wood only, and the sauce is either mustard based or vinegar and pepper based. And that is the long and the short of it. North Carolina has hickory wood, and they have on occasion been known to produce a good three rib down cross-breed hog. But your basic North Carolinians do not have good sense, because they will drench down that pork with ketchup-based sauce and that will not do it.

As far as I'm concerned—and I have been a judge on many barbecue contests and do not treat it lightly—South Carolina barbecue is, and always has been, light years ahead of the rest of the country. Using smaller hogs—the three rib down category— and hickory wood and hickory coals, our barbecue will cross the finish line as tender as pound cake, and with our sauces and light bread and coleslaw and cold beer or lemonade, it will drop you to your knees, where you will weep tears of appreciation and never-ending gratitude. At the Springfield Frog Jump, the Irmo Okra Strut, and the Salley Chitlin Strut, I have seen serious men in business suits and full-grown Christian women go into what is called a "barbecue coma." So much for barbecue.

barbecue on the eastern seaboard. Call (843) 237–PIGG. Hours are 11:00 a.m. to 8:00 p.m. Friday through Saturday. Prices range from $4.50 to $7.00. There's more on Hog Heaven at www.hogheaven-bbq.com.

. Route 17 runs right through the heart of **Georgetown.** This is the third oldest city in South Carolina and is named after King George II. The entire district, which lies along the Sampit River and the white settlement of which dates back to the 1700s, is listed on the National Register of Historic Places. Long before the Revolutionary War, most of the wealth of the town came from indigo; later it came from rice. Today the two main industries are steel and paper production, but the old, deep harbor is still an important shipping port.

The *Red Store-Tarbox Warehouse* (very early eighteenth century) is a good spot to start your tour of this fascinating town. Originally this was part of a three-story brick tavern that also stored silks, indigo, and imported wines, as well as mail from English ships. The glamorous Theodosia Burr Allston, daughter of Aaron Burr, sailed from this wharf in 1812 and was never seen again. Her husband, the governor of South Carolina, died of grief, or so the story goes.

Harborwalk is a 1,000-foot-long, 12-foot-wide boardwalk at the edge of the Sampit River. Along this walk are the back-door entrances and pastel awnings of the Front Street shops and restaurants. This is a delightful place to stroll and get your bearings. Three of the restaurants on Front Street look out over the boardwalk and water. The *River Room* at 801 Front is known for its excellent seafood salads, homemade french-fried onion rings, and its iced tea served in wide-mouthed Mason jars. Prices are from $6.00 to $12.00 for lunch. Dinner prices range from $6.00 to $19.95. Call (843) 527–4110.

Also on Front Street—you can't miss it—is the *Town Clock/Old Market* at 633 Front Street. Call (843) 546–7423. Built in 1835, this tower was used as a marketplace, city hall, and lockup. Today it houses the *Rice Museum* on the second floor. It displays the history of the rice empire that flourished here in the nineteenth century. Admission is $4.00 for seniors, $5.00 for adults, $2.00 for students ages twelve to twenty-one, and free for children under twelve who are accompanied by an adult. Call (843) 546–7423. Check out www.ego .net/us/sc/myr/rice.

Across the street is the Georgetown Chamber of Commerce at 10010 Front Street. Call (843) 546–8436. This is also a good spot to start a tour of the older sections of town. Here you can get maps, tourist information, schedules, and a list of bed-and-breakfasts in the area. Visit www.georgetowncountychamber .com.

Be sure to pick up a Georgetown National Register Historic District Map. Since there are forty-four historic sites all within a comfortable walking distance, I'd suggest simply starting off from the chamber with the map in your hand and following the numbers. Some truly delightful houses are on this walking tour.

A typical house on the tour is the **Harold Kaminski House** at 1003 Front Street. Call (843) 546–7706. Among those who lived here was Captain Dagget, a local hero who built the mine that sank the Union flagship *Harvest Moon* in Winyah Bay in 1865. Today the house has an outstanding collection of antiques from various periods.

The Georgetown Ice Company, 300 North Fraser Street, a low, rambling filling station that has, over the years, turned into the biggest convenience store in the state, is a one-of-a-kind South Carolina wonder. Drop by for a beer or a Blenheim Ginger Ale. This store caters to anglers, hunters, and anyone and everyone passing through. They sell everything, and you'll be hard pressed to name something they don't have. The range is incredible: fishing rods, tackle, worms, crickets, minnows, hot dogs, clothing, magazines, gas, oil, groceries, pharmaceuticals, boiled peanuts, et cetera, et cetera, et cetera. If you're from the north country, give boiled peanuts a chance. They'll seem vile at first, but they will definitely grow on you. Every time I go to New York City, my friends there beg me to bring them a few large sacks. Call (843) 546–6169 if you want to, but there's no need to phone: They are open twenty-four hours a day, seven days a week.

The best bet for rooms downtown is the **Carolinian Inn** at 706 Church Street. The rooms are pleasant and beautifully kept, and connecting rooms for when you're traveling with kids are available. The outdoor pool is surrounded by palm trees and a brick wall that keeps the breezes down, meaning you can swim almost any time. Continental breakfast is complimentary. Rates vary from $59 to $84. Call (843) 546–5191. You can even book a room online at www .carolinianinn.com.

Directly across the street is the **Lafayette Restaurant,** 532 Church Street, open six days a week from 5:00 a.m. to 10:00 p.m. This is a very, very popular spot for breakfast, among anglers in particular. Try it. They have a way of serving you your eggs and bacon and grits and toast all at the same time. In other words, the toast is not getting cold while the rest of the meal is coming. The coffee is great; so are the waitresses. Go there and, when you get back home, spread the word that this is the place for the perfect breakfast. Call (843) 546–5033.

Blackwater Adventures is headed by Louis Nexus, a native with more than twenty years' experience in guiding people through the rivers and inlets in this area. Louis is strongly behind preserving and promoting the natural environment of South Carolina. He offers a trip called the **Low Country**

Sampler, a six- to seven-hour canoe trip that includes lunch and a choice of skeet shooting or freshwater fishing. The trip costs $65 for adults and is free for children age twelve and under. Another trip, the *Pinopolis Dam Lock System Tour,* allows you to see the largest single-step dam lock in the world, with a drop of 75 feet. Through the Santee Cooper Lake System (which were the largest artificial lakes in the world until the Aswan Dam was completed), this guided canoe trip provides some unforgettable scenery. Other exclusive trips and overnights in the area can be made by arrangement. Group discounts are also available. Call (800) 761–1850 for inquiries and reservations. Write them at P.O. Box 4639, Pinopolis 29469. Or visit www.blackwateradventure.com.

Carolina Safari is as eclectic as its tour director, Virgil Graham, who is an area native, a naturalist, and a magazine photographer. The mailing address is Carolina Safari, P.O. Box 6799, Myrtle Beach 29577. On the jeep tours of various sites in the Low Country, you will see egrets, bald eagles, alligators, maritime fossils, and a variety of ecosystems, including saltwater marshes, cypress swamps, and more. Narrative background on Indian, colonial, and antebellum history is offered along with examples of 300-year-old plantations, Drunken Jack's Island, and visits to other legendary haunts of the Low Country

The jeeps are genuine, customized safari-style touring vehicles that seat ten to twelve people, and each one has a driver/guide. Binoculars are provided, stops are frequent and spontaneous, and you can take photos from any seat. Three-hour tours are offered daily at a cost of $30 for adults and $15 for children under age twelve. Pickup is available at most resorts and condos. Special tours and group rates can be arranged. Call (843) 497–5330 for reservations and further information. Or visit www.carolinasafari.com.

Andrews Old Town Hall Museum, 12 West Main Street, is open Tuesday and Thursday only, from 10:00 a.m. until 4:00 p.m. or by appointment. The museum is located in the town of Andrews, inland 18 miles west of Georgetown on Route 521. Representing a typical Victorian-era Andrews home, everything in the museum is circa 1909, the year Andrews was founded. Included are a child's room with period toys, a complete kitchen, and a Victorian parlor with period furniture, pictures, a pump organ, and a Victrola. Also depicting 1909 life are a complete Victorian schoolroom and a farm shed with tools, scales, harnesses and traces, hogshead containers, a plow, and plow points. Call (843) 264–3471. For more, see www.lowcountry-sc.com/andrews/oldtown.htm.

North of Georgetown a few miles, you're in *Pawleys Island* country. The bumper stickers on the cars of some of the summer inhabitants say ARROGANTLY SHABBY. Despite this cloying little observation, the people are friendly and the island is a one-of-a-kind gem. Many of the beach houses have been here since long before the Civil War.

Just staying on Pawleys Island for a week or so is in itself a perfect vacation, but there is much more to do here than just bake in the sun and watch for porpoises. Take fishing, specifically surf fishing. You need no license, and you can fish literally anywhere on the beach where you can cast a line. Surf fishing starts in the spring and the favorite spots are right here: the south end of Litchfield Beach, the south and north end of Pawleys, and the south end of Garden City Beach. All of these run together, so there's no trouble finding your way. For surf fishing you'll need a surf rod, which you can buy or rent from almost any store in Pawleys. The rod should be between 8 and 11 feet long with an open-face saltwater reel, filled with 10- to 20-pound test mono-filament line. You should also have two or three bottom-rig end tackles with three-ounce pyramid sinkers and 2/0 hooks. You'll need a sand spike to hold your rod, some fresh mullet cut in 1-inch pieces, sunglasses, a cooler filled with your favorite drinks, a beach towel or chair to sit on, and a good book to read.

Why the book? In the spring, three major species of fish are in the surf: sea trout, red drum that have moved out of the estuaries, and bluefish that are moving north along the coast. If any of these fish happen to be feeding, you can get all kinds of action. If the fish haven't arrived at your spot on the beach or have just passed by, you'll have plenty of time to read.

No one really knows what happens when you're sitting in a beach chair with your feet in the water and a surf rod sticking in a sand spike, but it seems that life definitely slows down and down and down. Up and down the end-less beach you'll see the young and the old, the fat and the slim doing it all day, every day. But it's not all just sitting there. Every half hour or so you can rise up, crank in the line, and then cast it out again. Then you can sit back down.

If you enjoy this kind of serenity, stop at **Pawleys Island Supplies,** 10460 Ocean Highway (843–237–2912) on Route 17, rent some equipment, and come on down.

If surf fishing and surf sitting aren't dramatic enough for you, you can charter a boat at Georgetown and head out for the Gulf Stream 60 miles away to try your luck with white marlin, blue marlin, dolphin, wahoo, or yellowfin tuna. All fishing tackle and bait are furnished, and you'll have a skilled but expensive captain with radar equipment for spotting the fish and getting you there. The bad news on the price is that it can run as high as $1,200 for the day and you need at least a week for reservations. The good news is that you can take along five buddies, which comes out to $200 each.

While you're out in the Gulf Stream, the temperature will be hotter (more than one hundred degrees), the water will be greener, and you'll see clumps

Fighting Stallions, Brookgreen Gardens

of fern and kelp and whole stalks of coconut trees drifting by from as far away as Barbados. You might fish all day and not get a single strike. But then again you might hook into an 800-pound tarpon or a 400-pound sailfish or find yourself plowing through a school of 200-pound amberjack.

Brookgreen Gardens, a former indigo and rice plantation, is an outdoor sculpture garden, located on Route 17 at Murrells Inlet. It was originally purchased by Archer and Anna Hyatt Huntington as a setting for their art collection. It is now acclaimed as the world's finest collection of American figurative sculpture. If you like the work of Remington, you'll like this. One particular piece will please the kids: a life-size sculpture of an alligator by David Turner. The current total number of pieces in the collection is 547 works by 241 artists; the collection is still growing. At the entrance is the powerful *Fighting Stallions* by famed sculptress Anna Hyatt Huntington; it is the largest sculpture ever cast in aluminum. This entire garden, with its incredible expanse of grass and beautiful landscape and wildlife, is well worth the visit. While here, you will also get an idea of how a plantation should look. The 9,127 acres of Brookgreen Gardens extend from the beachfront on the Atlantic Ocean to the freshwater swamps along the Waccamaw River. The garden's paths are laid out in the shape of a butterfly, and flowers bloom here from early spring right into September. The Terrace Cafe on the grounds overlooks a truly wonderful view of the park and the woods; it serves sandwiches, salads, soups, and snacks. Picnic facilities are located opposite the sculpture gardens' parking lot, next to Jessamine Park. This is the perfect spot for a picnic and is a delightful place to spend several hours. Once again, pack your favorite insect repellent and be prepared for deer flies and no-see-ums. A gift shop here offers gifts, books, and items that tell the story of Brookgreen Gardens. Admission here is $12.00 for adults, $10.00 for young adults ages thirteen to eighteen, and $5.00 for children age twelve. Open daily from 9:30 a.m. to 5:00 p.m. Call (843) 237-4218 more at www.brookgreen.org.

Belle Isle and Battery White originally belonged to Revolutionary hero Peter Horry, for whom Horry County is named. Battery White, an earthen Confederate fortification, was built on the plantation overlooking the bay for the defense of Georgetown during the Civil War. A short distance offshore lies the sunken Union flagship *Harvest Moon,* which went down during the last days of Georgetown's Union occupation when a Confederate bomb planted on board went off. The entrance to Belle Isle, now a resort community, is located south of Georgetown on South Island Road off Route 17. There is no charge to visit Battery White. For access, go to the Belle Isle guard gate, which is clearly marked on Route 17.

Due to the popularity of the *Yawkey Wildlife Center* tour, located at .1 Yawkey Way South in Georgetown, reservations must be made three to six months in advance. Call (843) 546–6814 or contactwww.yawkeyfoundation .org. Accessible only by boat, the Yawkey preserve consists of North and South Island and most of Cat Island, three coastal islands at the mouth of Winyah Bay. Willed to the state wildlife department by the late Tom Yawkey, who owned the Boston Red Sox, the center is dedicated to the management of waterfowl habitat. In cooperation with other state agencies, this center was largely responsible for saving the brown pelican a few years back. Today these birds are no longer on the endangered species list. As a matter of fact, if you're on almost any of the islands down here, you can count as many as fifty or sixty brown pelicans in a single formation as they fly home in the evening.

The Hammock Shop, 10880 Ocean Highway at Pawleys Island, is open year-round, Monday through Saturday from 10:00 a.m. to 6:00 p.m. and Sunday from 1:00 to 5:00 p.m.; summer hours are 9:30 a.m. to 8:00 p.m. from mid-June through August. Call (843) 237–9122. Since 1938 this has been a favorite destination down here in the Low Country for shoppers. Originally set up to make and sell rope hammocks, they now sell cookbooks, clothing, and beachwear, as well as another hundred items to take home as gifts. One of their most popular items is their famous rope hammocks, which you can see being made right before your eyes. If you want solid comfort and absolutely no danger of falling out, get the wider version, which can accommodate two people or four or five dogs. You can check out their entire catalog at www .hammockshop.com.

The Hammock Shop's charming *Tyler's Cove* restaurant specializes in fresh seafood and Low Country cuisine. It also offers weekly specials and a raw/steamed seafood bar. At *Sweet Temptations* you can get homemade candies, cookies, taffy, and pastries as well as delicious soups, salads, and deli sandwiches. Be sure to stop at the *Pawleys Island Ice Cream Shop,* too. Finally, *The Hammock Shop General Store* is truly a wonderful and

Fishing: The Party Boat

Of all of the sport-fishing boats that smoke out of Murrells Inlet heading for the Gulf Stream 60 miles out in search of marlin, tuna, and the great white shark, the bottom of the line is the party boat. This is a big iron monster that resembles a locomotive and stretches out 80 to 90 feet, with metal tubes every 18 inches for holding your rods. Standing side by side with another 130 customers, you get the feeling that you are chained together on a slave ship bound for some Dutch possession. Leaving the harbor, the boat throws up a wake so big other anglers scream and shake their fists. But despite the crowd, and the perfunctory way you are treated, the party boat is the only fishing boat that posts the sign:

WE GUARANTEE—YOU WILL CATCH FISH! OR YOUR MONEY BACK!

imaginative gift store featuring a large collection of South Carolina books, recipes, and local ghost stories as well as bestsellers. If you want to take a gift to the folks back home, this is probably the best spot to shop on the coast.

Pawleys Island and Litchfield Beaches became, in a real sense, the first resort in America. Some say that malaria-bearing mosquitoes could not fly across the large salt marshes that separated the beaches from the mainland. Pawleys Island in particular became a favorite refuge for wealthy planter families, some of whose houses are still standing today. These planters also built large and lavish houses in Charleston and stayed there during the "social season" of February, which was after the crops were harvested. All the romantic images so often associated with the "Old South" and *Gone with the Wind* grew out of this period.

If you'd like to stay overnight here, and who wouldn't, stop by ***Pawleys Island-Litchfield Business Association*** on Route 17 at The Planter's Exchange. They'll show you a wide range of places to stay, including a 200-year-old beach house, a plantation manor house, bed-and-breakfasts, oceanfront hotel rooms and suites, and rooms and houses on the beach, on the creek, or on one of the many golf courses. For an overview, see www.pilba.org.

If you ignore the Route 17 bypass and stay on old Route 17, you'll go right through the heart of Murrells Inlet. Founded in the late eighteenth century by Captain Murrell, Murrells Inlet has supplied the Waccamaw Neck area with fresh seafood for over 200 years. Fleets of deep-sea fishing boats lie at anchor here and journey daily out to the Gulf Stream to bring back every possible kind of fish for the local restaurants.

Just off Murrells Inlet lies Drunken Jack's Island, where, according to local legend, a pirate named Jack was accidentally marooned with no provisions except his shipmates' excess rum supply. Months later, when the ship returned

Recipe for Corn Whiskey

These are the facts: (1) It's legal to make it; (2) it's illegal to sell it; (3) if it's made wrong, it will kill you.

Ingredients and equipment:

50 lbs. of corn meal
100 lbs. of sugar
One thick horse blanket
An old-fashioned hand-cranked clothes wringer

First we mix our meal and sugar in a fifty-gallon pot and pour in enough boiling water to fill it. Cover it for three days and nights or until it begins to "work." In the winter you may need an extra day. You then cook the mix—it is now called "mash." As it begins to cook, cover the pot with the horse blanket. After a half hour or so—depending on how hot you have your fire—the blanket will begin to sag with the steam. You then remove it and run it though the clothes wringer. What you see coming out is corn whiskey. It's not great corn whiskey, but it's corn whiskey nevertheless. It's also the perfect way a layman can understand the process. All whiskey stills operate on this basis. Every still—whether here in the Carolina pines or over in Scotland at the House of Johnny Walker—follows this same basic practice—mix their mash, cook it, catch the steam, and condense it. The rest is aging and advertising. Any questions?

to load up the rum cargo, all the crew found was case after empty case and spent rum bottles all along the shore, plus the bleached bones of poor Jack. The treasure of Blackbeard is also reputed to be buried here.

The highway meanders along under ancient live oaks by many unique seafood restaurants, ranging from old, weathered, time-honored culinary jewels with third-generation chefs and proprietors to more recent dining establishments with troubadours to delight the evening diners.

Perhaps the oldest and best-known dining spot is ***Oliver's Lodge,*** 4204 Route 17, Murrells Inlet, where they have been serving fresh fish, shrimp, and ribs since 1910. Everyone I know keeps going back and going back. When you go, insist on a table on the back porch overlooking the inlet. Dinners range from $15 to $25 and up. Open seven days a week. Call for reservations at (843) 651–2963.

Nance's Creek Front Restaurant at 4883 Highway 17 has a dining room with at least 100 feet of glass looking out over the marsh and the creek. The view is spectacular because you can see the boats coming in and going out and watch the changing colors on the marsh grass. The food is almost as good as the view. Prices are from $16 to $30. Open Monday through Saturday, 4:00 to 10:00 p.m., and 4:00 to 9:00 p.m. Sunday. Call (843) 651–2696.

Murrells Inlet is the absolute center for fishing down here. You can fish for almost anything you can imagine. As a matter of fact, the South Carolina coastline, creeks, and inland lakes probably offer a larger variety of fish than any place in the country. The only problem fish are the sharks and stingrays. Swimmers are warned to avoid large schools of fish, for the sharks feed among them. One sign of a shark feeding among fish is the presence of birds, which are waiting to scavenge the scraps.

The stingray is a bottom-dweller in the ocean and salt marshes. It won't attack, but its tail has a clever little barb that can cause a painful wound if it's stepped on. You are cautioned to shuffle your feet when wading in the water, so that they sense you coming and get out of your way. Be on the lookout for jellyfish and Portuguese man-of-wars. If they sting you, a quick remedy is to sprinkle the irritated area with meat tenderizer.

Along with charter-boat fishing for sport fish, there are two other types of fishing, namely, party-boat fishing and pier fishing. On the party boat you will certainly catch fish, but be prepared to put up with a few problems. Beer is sold on board, and, in the hot sun and after a night on the town, a few of your shipmates will be hooked over the rail doing you know what. To avoid having this happen to you, be sure to eat a very light and very dry breakfast. In other words, leave the grease alone. The trip is long—six hours. Once the big boat and its typically hundred-plus passengers leave the pier, there is no turning back. None, no matter what. On the other hand, it's cheap—$15 to $20 for six hours with rod and reel and bait all thrown in. If you can stand the heat, the captain, who knows the waters and the ways of the fish, will take you places where you can catch something. Children often have a better time here than adults.

If you don't want to get on board a party boat, the pier a couple miles north at Surfside is the easiest fishing in the world—and very pleasant. Here you can rent a rod and reel and buy bait and walk out on the half-mile pier to any seat you like. You cast your line in and sit back and enjoy the breeze. Pier fishers tend to be very agreeable people and will be pleased to answer any questions you have about bait and casting, and they may even identify what you might catch. Since most of the pier is lighted, many fishermen come carrying chaise lounges, blankets, coolers of food, and radios and stay all night. For regular daytime fishing you might catch anything from a blowfish to a shark. With a little luck, you can catch almost anything here if you're patient enough and the weather is right. Try to fish when the tide is coming in, not going out. When it's incoming, the fish follow it in to feed. The only problem you'll have out here if the fish are biting is that the kids will never want to come in.

Surfside Pier, just north of Murrells Inlet, is, at 800 feet, one of the longest fishing piers in the state. It's open twenty-four hours a day, seven days a week, and is lighted for night fishing. Prices are in the ballpark of $6.00 to rent a rod and reel, $7.00 to fish, and $4.00 for bait. Call the Surfside Pier at (843) 238–0121. Out on the end of the pier, many people fish with big rods and reels and often land spectacular catches. The record down here is a 128-pound tarpon that one George Singleton caught out on the end; he wore out a pair of shoes fighting the fish all the way back to the shore.

Surfside Pier is full of surprise catches. You'll see sand sharks, hammerheads, blowfish, and often a sheepshead as big as a good-size Labrador retriever. Down the middle of the pier are benches, and the old-timers staked out here are usually natives who can and will give you any information you want about the winds and the tides. They'll also be able to identify the strange creatures drawn up from the bottom. The sea robin is of particular interest—it has wings like a bat and a face like a catfish.

Almost everyone likes to talk and give advice down here. Take advantage of it. Take a long walk out to the end of the pier and ask anybody anything you want about fishing. It's amazing how much they know and how much there is to know. They will also tell you exactly what line, bait, and hook to use and exactly where to throw it in.

The Surfside Pier tackle shop has cold drinks, crackers, and so on, but for a very good meal at a fair price try *Nibil's,* right on the pier at 11 South Ocean Boulevard. The view up and down the beach and out over the Atlantic is especially nice in the mornings and evenings. Nibil's is open from 6:30 a.m. to 9:00 p.m. Monday through Saturday. Breakfast and lunch only are served on Sunday. The most popular breakfast is their country ham, grits, and eggs. Dinners range from $6.00 to $20.00; the specialties are fresh flounder, snapper, scallops, and Angus beef. The manager is Jack Cahill. He's outgoing and easy to talk to and knows just about everything there is to know about Surfside and the surrounding area. Call (843) 238–5080.

For fishing from the beach, all you need is a rod and reel, a chair, an umbrella, and a book to read. For bait use shrimp or squid or section up a small perch. Don't forget to bring along a hollow stake to hold up the pole.

South Carolina's Riviera

Ten miles north of Surfside you'll come to the outskirts of Myrtle Beach, an oasis that has been called everything from The Redneck Riviera to Blue Collar Mecca to Golfer's Heaven. Each of these descriptions fits like a glove. In February and March the Canadians swarm over the place, swim in the ocean, eat the all-you-can-eat breakfasts of pancakes, eggs, and bacon, and play eighteen holes in the morning and eighteen more in the afternoon. Most of them drive down. So if you see four men or four women wearing golf caps with the car trunk riding low with golf clubs and the roof rack piled high with golfing paraphernalia, they're heading for Myrtle Beach and they're harmless. To celebrate their arrival, the Myrtle Beach Chamber of Commerce floods the streets with Canadian flags, street-wide Canadian banners, and Canadian everything.

Figuring each golf course down here is approximately 5½ miles long and the South Carolina coastline has more than one hundred courses, the mathematics tell us that if you laid them end to end they would extend all the way from Little River, the northernmost point in South Carolina, across all of the Georgia coastline, and more than 200 miles into Florida. In other words, there are a lot of courses down here.

Golf is just one of the attractions here. Myrtle Beach sits on the very center of the Grand Strand, a 60-mile stretch of pristine beach that is uninterrupted by tidal inlets. Much of the beach slopes gently into the water and is ideal for kids, even small ones. Campers from everywhere are welcome here; the area provides more than 12,000 campsites. The Grand Strand is also the yearly after-graduation destination for thousands of high school kids who arrive every June for a week of beach music, walking up and down the promenade, hanging out at the Pavilion, and wide-open revelry.

Finally, Myrtle Beach has become a popular retirement spot for northerners who like the weather, the beach, the golf, the food, and the general laid-back attitude. Adding all these visitors together at the height of the season, the population soars to more than 350,000. But, despite the crush and heavy commercialization, you'll find nice touches of the Old South and friendly faces everywhere.

Ten miles north of Myrtle Beach on property now owned by the Myrtle Beach Hilton is **Arcadian Shores Golf Club.** This course, designed by Reis Jones, one of the premier golf architects on the scene today, combines the best of Mother Nature and the best of a modern golf course layout. The thirteenth and fourteenth holes, the signature holes, cross a cypress-studded lake that looks as if it's been here since the beginning of time. The tall pines, magnolias, and live oaks that frame the rest of the course create the perfect setting for the layout, which *Golf Magazine* and *Golf Digest* have placed in their top fifty year in and year out.

Since the purchase by the Hilton chain, guests here at the hotel have been granted preferential tee times, but the course is open year-round to guests staying in a number of other select hotels in the Myrtle Beach area. Arcadian Shores has recently been overhauled and improved. Now under the Hilton management, it has never been in better shape. For a weekend of top-flight golf, with a guaranteed tee time, only a few hundred yards from the Hilton,

you'll have to go a long way to beat Arcadian Shores. While staying at the Hilton, by the way, you can play almost any one of the sixty-odd courses within 30 miles of here. For information write to Arcadian Shores Golf Club, 701 Hilton Road, Myrtle Beach 29572, or call (843) 449–5217. Check out www.golfholiday .com/courses/arcadianshores.html.

Back down Route 17 you'll see signs for *The Dunes Golf and Beach Club.* This is the site of the annual Golf Writers of America Clambake, which is held every year one week before the Masters. Robert Trent Jones designed the holes in such a way that the wind hits golfers from every direction on the compass. What he has done is lived up to the old Scottish saying, "No wind, no golf."

The club and clubhouse are right on the ocean, with a beautiful view of the beach. The Dunes, probably the most famous course on the beach, is a must for golfing in South Carolina. Last year they hosted the U.S. Seniors Open. While the club is private, guests staying at a number of select hotels on the beach are allowed to play. So when you're making reservations, the first question you ask should not concern the rates, or if the room is on the ocean, or whether the bed comes equipped with Magic Fingers, but whether the hotel guarantees that you can play The Dunes. If it doesn't, tell them you'll call back. Then call the desk at The Dunes and ask them where you should stay. Call (843) 449–5236 or write The Dunes Golf and Beach Club, 9000 North Ocean Boulevard, Myrtle Beach 29572. Or visit www.dunesgolfandbeachclub.com.

Both The Dunes and Arcadian Shores abound with deer and raccoons. The rare fox squirrel—bigger than a regular squirrel and with a black mask around its eyes—is sometimes seen here. Watch for it. You might also see pileated woodpeckers, alligators, and an occasional armadillo. Recently there have been several sightings of the South Florida manatee.

Years ago, the hotel and golf course owners put Myrtle Beach on the map with the introduction of the "golf package." Until then, golf resorts ran themselves like exclusive country clubs. This practice is still prevalent in most of the country, but down here the owners have gotten together to make golf not only available but affordable. As a consequence, when you check in at a hotel you are automatically guaranteed golf course privileges on almost any of

Cooking Fish

You scale it, clean it, load it down with cracker crumbs, and lay it gently in 550-degree grease. You turn it once. Only once. The fish is done when it looks done.

On fried fish, which is the best fish, down here we eat everything—the tail, the dorsal fin, the mouth, head, eyes, and all. The cats, returning to some ancient savagery, dispose of the darker organs, then calm down to clean and polish the bones. And since any walking hound prefers fish bones to pork chop and chicken bones, the rest goes out on the step for Old Trailer and his youngest son, Boomer. In short, the cooking of fish, like of the hog and the Great Plains buffalo, is ecologically perfect; there is no waste. Fish scales are scalloped around the GOD BLESS OUR MORTGAGED HOME signs and, in the hands of an inspired artist, gilded gold and blue and magenta to liven up the seashell memorabilia that crowd the mantels from Cocoa Beach to the Outer Banks along the North Carolina coast.

the courses in the area. Golf packages, high-quality courses, and the weather have combined to make Myrtle Beach the most popular golf destination in the world.

BUT! There's always a but. You can't just check into any hotel and get the full golf package. So you'll have to do a little spadework to find out exactly what courses are available on your particular package.

Choosing a hotel and golf package is easier with the help of the Myrtle Beach Chamber of Commerce. Call them at (800) 356–3016, or write Myrtle Beach Area Chamber of Commerce, P.O. Box 2115, Myrtle Beach 29578. They'll send you, free of charge, an elaborate 313-page magazine of hotel, golf course, restaurant, and nightclub information. Called the Stay & Play Guide, it can answer all of your questions about where to stay and exactly which golf courses come with each package. You can also visit www.mbchamber.com.

Barefoot Landing, 4898 Highway 17 South, North Myrtle Beach, is a 120-shop-and-restaurant complex built on and out over the Intracoastal Waterway. The shops and restaurants here are constructed of weathered cypress-like wood and decorated with bright green awnings. Children can ride a European-style carousel. The entire area is pleasant to stroll around and watch the ducks and the big fish in the river. Children love this area and can be turned loose to explore. Call (800) 272–2320. Check out www.bflanding.com.

A great spot to have a cold one at night on Barefoot Landing on Route 17, 11 miles south of the North Carolina border, is the famous *House of Blues* at 4640 Highway 17 South. This is the number one spot in South Carolina for blues. One of the big stars here, from Pomaria, South Carolina, is Nathanial Nappy Brown who is a one-of-a-kind wonder. Nappy wrote many of the hot blues numbers that are still with us. He has been, and still is, friends with Chuck Berry, B. B. King, The Beatles, et cetera, and doesn't mind sitting down with you and telling you everything he knows about them and their music. The restaurant is open from 8:00 a.m. until 9:00 or 10:00 p.m. daily. Ticket prices are $30 for a full meal and show. Call (843) 272–3000.

The Dixie Stampede is a 1,000-seat theater owned by Dolly Parton. The added attraction here is you can eat a full meal while you watch the show. These shows are one of the biggest successes in the area and keep getting bigger and bigger. If you come down, be sure to catch at least one. Frankly, they are all a little bit the same. But that's all right, because the stars are all professionals and go all out to put on a good show. The theaters are high tech and state of the art. Between acts performers sit on the edge of the stage and talk to the crowd. The price is $40.03 for adults. For reservations and information call (800) 433–4401. Check out www.dixiestampede.com.

Myrtle Beach is the Putt-Putt Capital of the known world. It also has a 20,000-square-foot wave pool, and for a few bucks you can take a helicopter ride around the area or parasail up and down the beach.

Ristorante Villa Romana at 707 South King's Highway, Myrtle Beach, is open for dinner seven days a week. A delightful place to dine, Villa Romana has strolling violinists and a gypsy accordionist. Often Mama Lucia, overcome by Puccini or Verdi, will dance and sway among the tables. The specialties here are traditional Italian recipes; they serve probably the best veal in the area. The soups, pasta, and bread are all made fresh daily. Prices range from $17 to $30. Call (843) 448–4990. Or check out www.villaromanamyrtlebeach.com.

Myrtle Beach State Park, located at 4401 South King's Highway, is one of forty-eight state parks in South Carolina. Call (843) 238–5325. Currently the

More Golf Advice

Pro-Fit Inc., owned and operated by Mike Harris at 1616 Highway 17 South in North Myrtle Beach, (843) 361–0102, is a must stop for all serious golfers. Mike, a genuine wizard with every aspect of golf, has an amazing discovery that you must try out. For no charge he will test your clubs on a frequency vibration machine. There is a strong chance even the best and most expensive club shafts aren't matched properly. Mike will show you which ones are not in sync with the others, then he'll match them with the rest of the clubs and sell you what you need at a very moderate price. When all your clubs have the same frequency, only then are they truly matched, and only then can you swing with the same swing. While this is no guarantee to bring your handicap down, it will do wonders for your confidence, which after all is what the golf swing is all about. It works for me.

Music

Not only is South Carolina the birthplace of Beach Music and such groups as The Platters, The Coasters, and The Drifters, it's right up there at the top in blues and bluegrass. For blues, try the House of Blues at Barefoot Landing. As for bluegrass, it's best on an AM station, preferably on one of the hundred back roads that don't make the cut on most maps. If you hear the same music in a New York or Chicago traffic jam, it's just not the same. It's not even close. But when you get on some old Carolina tar-and-gravel road, with the mules and the cotton and the R.U. READY FOR ETERNITY painted on automobile tires and nailed to the fence posts, and the dogs are all standing around in threes and fours, I guarantee it's going to make a big, big difference. Don't laugh until you try it.

following accommodations are available here in the Myrtle Beach area: five cabins (each sleeps six) at $73.37 during the summer, per cabin per night, and $52.56 off-season, per cabin per night; two apartments (each sleeps four) at $48.18 per night during the summer and $42.71 per night off-season; and 350 campsites at $22.00 a night from April 1 through October 31 and $18.60 a night from November 1 through March 31. Prices subject to change. Call for current rates. To make reservations online, visit www.southcarolinaparks.reserveamerica.com.

If you would like further information on any or all of the forty-eight parks in the state, please write South Carolina State Parks, c/o Kay White, 1205 Pendelton Street, Columbia 29201. The parks are famous for their fireplace-equipped cabins, their beautiful settings, nature hikes, golf courses, and fishing expeditions. Needless to say, this is a nonprofit operation, and it offers a wonderful way to visit and vacation at very reasonable prices.

Downtown in Myrtle Beach in the heart of the heart of it all is **Ripley's Believe It or Not** (901 North Ocean Boulevard). If you haven't been here yet, don't miss it this time. It's endless, incomprehensible, and amazing.

Some of the hotter tickets at Ripley's are "Three-Ball Charlie"—the man who could put three balls in his mouth (tennis ball, golf ball, billiard ball) and whistle at the same time—a genuine Jivaro shrunken head from Ecuador, a two-headed calf, and a mock graveyard with an R.I.P. stone engraved:

HERE LIES AN ATHEIST,

ALL DRESSED UP AND

NO PLACE TO GO.

And who could forget "Kamala, the wolf girl, raised in the jungles of India by wolves."

Kids love this place; if you let them, they'll stay here all day. Prices are $11.95 for adults, $7.95 for kids ages six to twelve, free for kids five and under. If you save your ticket, you get a dollar off on a pizza next door at *The Pizza Place.* Ripley's is open 10:00 a.m. to 8:00 p.m. daily year-round. Call (843) 448–2331.

Across the street, at 916 North Boulevard, is the *Gay Dolphin Incorporated,* which simply defies description. You literally have to go here to believe it. Every conceivable shell design, every T-shirt, every possible item of tacky and not-so-tacky mantelpiece memorabilia, whatnot, wall hanging, and bumper sticker in the Western world is here. And the place is cavernous. My favorite bumper sticker is I DON'T CALL 911. They also carry some pretty funny postcards. One is a pitch-black card with the caption "Myrtle Beach at Midnight." Be sure to stop here. It's a standing bet, even money, that you won't leave until you buy something. Summer hours (Easter through Labor Day) are 9:30 a.m. to 11:30 p.m. Sunday through Thursday, and 9:30 a.m. until midnight Friday and Saturday. After Labor Day, open daily 9:00 a.m. to 5:30 p.m. Call (843) 448–6550.

There are a couple of house rules on Myrtle Beach. Dogs must be on a leash at all times. No animals are allowed on the beach or Ocean Boulevard between Twenty-first Avenue North and Thirteenth Avenue South during any time of the year. No dogs are allowed on the beach between 9:00 a.m. and 5:00 p.m. from May 15 through September 15.

Riding horses on the beach is allowed from November 12 through February 27. A few miles south, at Surfside, you can ride from November 2 through March 31.

Up on the end of Route 17 is the Little River area, which is famous for Calabash-style seafood and a wealth of brand-new and exciting golf courses. Right in the middle of Little River is *Tidewater Golf Club and Plantation,* named in 1990 the best new public course in the country by *Golf Magazine* and *Golf Digest.* Once again, this is a public course open to almost anyone with a set of sticks. All you have to do is call (843) 249–3829 for a tee time and bring plenty of balls for the water holes.

The great secret of Tidewater's unique success lies with Ken Tomlinson, the owner and course designer. He has laid out multiple landing areas for each tee, a design feature that allows players of every level to play the same iron from fairway to green on each hole. Another of Ken's wise decisions here at Tidewater is that he has given the course the best land possible—the high, wooded peninsula that lies between the Atlantic Ocean and the Intracoastal Waterway. And still another feature of the course is that Ken doesn't believe in the dreary ninety-degree use of carts on the fairways. On most days you can drive them right down the middle and save yourself a lot of club carrying and unnecessary walking. Ken says, "Hell, it's only grass." This is a superb course and it stays in beautiful shape. For further information write Tidewater Golf Club and Plantation, 4901 Little River Neck Road, North Myrtle Beach 29582. Call (800) 446–5363, or fax (843) 249–5281. You can investigate their golf packages at www.tide-water.com.

On Route 501 past Conway and Aynor, you'll come to the **Galivants Ferry Convenience Store,** 3842 Joyner Swamp Road. Right here is the center for the 114-year-old stump-meeting convention that occurs here every June. The organizer is one John Monroe Holliday, who also oversees the largest tobacco farm in operation in South Carolina as well as a number of diverse business interests throughout Horry County.

In 1979 the Hollidays were honored for their contribution to the economic progress of the area and for their public service to South Carolina by the Department of Highways and Public Transportation. The section of U.S. Highway 501 between Galivants Ferry and Conway was renamed The Holliday Highway.

John Holliday, his brother Joseph, and their families have been personally responsible for continuing a tradition their grandfather began in 1880—The Galivants Ferry Democratic Stump Speaking. John Holliday says, "I remember sitting on a wagon in a thicket, drinking cherry cola while fifty to seventy-five people stood on a stump or some boards to speak. The Stump started when there was only a Democratic party in the state. We didn't even know how to spell Republican."

John and his brother Joseph have continued another tradition started by their grandfather. Each of them has been the postmaster of Galivants Ferry.

A stop here at the convenience store right on the highway and a chance to meet John Holliday or one of his family, who will tell you all about the place and certainly invite you to the June meeting, is definitely a once-in-a-lifetime experience.

The **Original Benjamin's Calabash Seafood and Nautical Museum,** located at 9593 North Kings Highway, Myrtle Beach, is a one-of-a-kind masterpiece. It offers a 170-item buffet with crab legs; Asian, Italian, and country food; seafood, soup, salad, and dessert bars. It can seat and serve over 500 guests at a time. As you first enter the restaurant, you will see the world's largest model of the *Queen Elizabeth,* the actual one that was shown to the queen before the ship was built in her honor. Next you will see the dry sea aquarium, which houses the largest collection of mounted fish in the Southeast. As advertised, all the fish were alive at one time. You will also see the largest replica of the *Mayflower.* The rest of the lobby and the many rooms that make up

Benjamin's Original Calabash are filled with compasses, telescopes, underwater cameras, buoys, anchors, aquariums, and much, much more. There is also a full-sized shark hanging outside the front door. In other words, Benjamin's Calabash Restaurant has to be seen to be believed. And the food and service is probably the best on the beach.

Caution, this is the original **Benjamin's Calabash.** There are other Calabashes along the beach, and a few are even using the names Ben and Benjamin's. But in the words of the circus, "Be not deceived by envious competitors." All you have to do is try the Original Benjamin's and you will stray no farther. For reservations call (800) 288–8687. Open daily May through September from 2:30 p.m. to whenever dinner is over. Open at 3:30 p.m. from October through April. For further information, visit Benjamin's at www.original benjamins.com.

Another fine inn on the beach is **The Islander Inn** at 57 West First Street, Ocean Isle Beach, offering the very finest lodging, accommodations, and expert assistance for the golf enthusiast. Highly recommended are the Pearl Course and Angels Trace. I've played both, and they are outstanding. The inn features indoor and outdoor pools as well as a first-class spa. In case you think you're too far north of South Carolina, keep in mind you're only 10 miles from Little River. Call them at (888) 325–4753 or (910) 575–7000; fax (910) 575–7075; www.islanderinn.com.

Stop at **Victoria's Restaurant and Sports Bar** at 125 Causeway Drive, for homemade crab cakes and snow crab legs. They also serve a delicious 12-ounce rib eye and 10-ounce filet mignon. This casual neighborhood watering hole comes complete with dart boards, pool table, and eleven—count them—TV screens. A great spot to relax, eat, and watch your favorite game. Live entertainment on weekends. Open daily; call (910) 575–4746 for hours.

The Museum of Coastal Carolina, the area's premier museum of natural history, is located at 21 East Second Street. It is an ideal place to bring the family, especially the kids. Every day at 2:00 p.m. there is a nature program and/or storytime. Topics include snakes, alligators, fossils, shells, birds of prey, fish and fishing, and Native American lore. For small children, there is a hands-on-activity area, complete with bones, shells, skulls, hides, and magnification devices. In addition there is a Loggerhead Turtle Watch every evening at 7:00 p.m. Open Monday through Saturday 9:00 a.m. to 5:00 p.m. and Sunday 1:00 to 5:00 p.m. Call (910) 579–1016. Visit their Web site at www.museumofcc.org.

Goose Creek Bed and Breakfast at 1901 Egret Street is perfectly located right in the heart of Ocean Isle. There is a pier that gives you access to fishing and, if you bring a canoe or a kayak, you can fish the waters of the Intracoastal Waterway. What better way to spend a vacation? Rates range from $80 to $100 per night in-season and $70 to $90 per night off-season. Special golf packages are available. Call (800) 275–6540 or visit www.goosecreekbb.com.

Ten miles north of Ocean Isle, go to Southport and pick up the ferry to one of the most amazing and most beautiful islands in the Atlantic—***Bald Head Island,*** North Carolina. Departing from Indigo Plantation on West Ninth Street in Southport (910–457–5003), you will go out to the island, go on the tour, have lunch, and return. The fee is $15.00 per adult, $8.00 per child under twelve. While out on Bald Head, you can look over the very fine golf course and the accommodations, see the famous Old Baldy Lighthouse, and decide when you want to come back to spend a few days. Most of this remarkable island has been given over to the state wildlife commission and is now a bird and turtle sanctuary. It also has one of the finest stands of live oaks and maritime forests on the coast. Pelicans and giant herons are everywhere, and at night there is a good chance you will see a loggerhead. Another bonus is that there are no cars except maintenance vehicles. If you are going to do one thing and one thing only in North Carolina, here's what you do. Go to Bald Head, play eighteen holes on the truly great course lined with live oaks, herons, egrets, pelicans, and almost any kind of wildlife you can imagine. Then have a cool one at the bar overlooking the rocks and surf while you watch the sun slowly set, and luxuriously reflect on what a great day it has been and how you might just very well stay. A good place to start looking for information is www.baldheadislandinformation.com.

A Sample of North Carolina

Let's face it, Myrtle Beach is getting crowded. So is North Myrtle Beach. If you want to play golf, stay at a great place, be on the ocean, and get away from the traffic and bustle, all you have to do is drive 8 to 10 miles north of **Tidewater Golf Club and Plantation** in Little River (see description earlier in this section). You can cross the North Carolina line without a passport. And the natives are friendly.

A great spot to stop and look around would be **Ocean Isle Beach and the Ocean Isle Inn,** at 37 West First Street. Call (800) 352–5988 or (910) 579–0750. From here you are within ten minutes of thirty-six championship golf courses in North and South Carolina and some of the finest food and fishing in the world. Unlike most East Coast beaches, which run north-south, Ocean Island is east-west oriented, which lets you see some of the most incredible sunrises and sunsets imaginable. This is the perfect place for family vacations, reunions, club outings, or romantic getaways.

The premier course here is the **Ocean Isle Beach Golf Course,** where I have played many times. I am here to tell you, it's wonderful. For more information, call (910) 579–2610.

Nearby at Highway 301 and Interstate 95 in Hamer is South of the Border (or SOB, as it's known to insiders), an amalgam of South Carolina and Old Mexico—a yellow and pink Tijuana backed in black velvet. Pedro, a 97-foot statue, straddles the entrance and is billed as "the largest freestanding sign east of the Mississippi." You can drive in between his legs. Inside they have the biggest, brightest, tackiest assortment of what is affectionately called memorabilia, which runs the gamut from eight types of back-scratchers to at least thirty, and still counting, types of coffee mugs. They also have flags of every description, clever bumper stickers, tapes, CDs, and woodcuts of "God Bless Our Mortgaged Home."

Under Pedro's magnificent sombrero, billed as the Eiffel Tower of the South, dozens of weddings take place every summer. For $160 you can get married and spend a night in an "heir-conditioned" honeymoon suite complete with champagne, a water bed, and a free breakfast, which isn't a bad way to start a married life. South Carolinians claim they wouldn't be caught dead here, but the place is packed, and if you want a room, you'll have to call in advance for a reservation. Call (843) 774–2411. Visit their Web site at www.pedroland .com, but don't expect it to be "politically correct."

Places to Stay in the Grand Strand

GEORGETOWN

Mansfield Plantation
1776 Mansfield Road
(843) 546–6961
www.mansfieldplantation
.com

Shaw House
613 Cypress Court
(843) 546–9663
www.bbonline.com/sc/
shawhouse

MYRTLE BEACH

Serendipity Inn
407 71st Avenue North
(843) 449–5268
www.serendipityinn.com

PAWLEYS ISLAND

Litchfield Plantation
P.O. Box 320
(843) 237–5300
www.litchfield.com

Places to Eat in the Grand Strand

MURRELLS INLET

Inlet House Cafe
Highway 17 Murrells Inlet
(843) 651–0622

Nance's Creek Front Restaurant
Highway 17 Business
(843) 651–2696

Oliver's Lodge
4204 Highway 17 Business
(843) 651–2963

Tyler's Cove Restaurant
727 Wachesaw Road
(843) 651–5135

MYRTLE BEACH

Nibil's at Surfside
Pier 11 South Ocean
Boulevard
(843) 238–5080

The Fall Line

Tobacco and Cotton Lands

South Carolina is roughly a triangle covering 30,000 square miles, 500 of which are inland lakes. From the northwest corner, near the Chattooga River, a rough and jagged line runs east for 330 miles to Little River Inlet, marking the boundary between South and North Carolina. To the west, the Savannah River extends southeast from that same northwest corner for 240 miles to Tybee Sound, which separates the state from Georgia and lies adjacent to Savannah. And on the east coast, the Atlantic shoreline stretches roughly 200 miles between Little River and Tybee Sound. The state is drained by three main river systems: the Pee Dee in the northeast, the Santee in the central area, and the Savannah in the southeast. The swift flow of the rivers in the Upcountry has led most of the state's manufacturing plants to select sites in that section. Below the Fall Line—which runs across the state and separates the Up from the Low—these red, mud-laden rivers become wide and clear, depositing their silt on the bottom. Stained black with tannic acid from cypress and other roots, the rivers run slowly under the live oaks and tupelos through the flat, rich soils to the Atlantic Ocean.

N. CAROLINA
S. CAROLINA

Cheraw

Lancaster

Bennettsville

TOBACCO AND
COTTON LANDS

Wateree
Lake

Winnsboro

Camden

Florence

N

Sumter

0   30 mi
0   30 km

N. Fk. Edisto R.

Aiken S. Fk. Edisto R.

Orangeburg

Lake
Marion

S. CAROLINA
GEORGIA

REVOLUTIONARY

WAR COUNTRY

Barnwell

Savannah R.

The area in the northeast around the muddy Pee Dee River is called the Pee Dee section, and right in the middle is the city of **Florence.** The city is in the heart of the tobacco region of the state, and every fall the annual Tobacco Jubilee is an important event of the Pee Dee Fair. A visit to the city, which is 65 miles from the coast, is interesting in that it shows how an old downtown section of a small town can still compete with a brand-new sprawling mall a few miles away.

Barringer Hardware, on Evans Street, is about 150 feet deep, and every square inch is covered with merchandise. Fan belts and parts of plows hang from rafters, and if you look hard enough you can find two different sizes of old-fashioned scrub boards for washing clothes. Jack Barringer, the owner, also sells fireplace equipment, copper tubing, wet mops, paints, iron skillets, about two dozen different kinds of brushes, and a galvanized double tub suitable for bathing a not-very-large person. Up in his office he has a poster from years ago advertising buggy and wagon parts. Jack is easygoing and easy to talk to. If you have any questions about Florence, he'll be glad to answer them.

Florence has been nicknamed "Tooth City," "Tooth Capital," and "Denture Capital of the World" due to the reputation of the **Sexton Dental Clinic,** at 377 West Palmetto Street. It advertises "affordable general dentistry," so people come from as far away as Hawaii and Alaska because of the low prices and the fact that work is done by the assembly-line method and almost anything, even full dentures top and bottom, can be done right here in one day. They're open

AUTHOR'S FAVORITE PLACES

The Chitlin Strut
Salley
www.chitlinstrut.com

Darlington Raceway
Darlington
www.darlingtonraceway.com

Florence Museum of Art, Science, and History
558 Spruce Street
Florence
(843) 662-3351
www.florencemuseum.org

Palmetto Golf Club
Aiken
www.palmettogolfclub.net
(803) 649-2951

Springfield Frog Jump
Springfield
(803) 258-3152

Swan Lake Iris Gardens
Sumter
(803) 775-1231

Willcox Inn
100 Colleton Avenue
Aiken
(800) 434-6835

Monday through Friday from 7:00 a.m. to 5:00 p.m. For emergencies, they are open twenty-four hours a day, seven days a week. They accept major credit cards. Call (843) 662–2543. Their Web site is www.sextondental.net.

At lunchtime, head to **Red Bone Alley** at 1903 West Palmetto Street. This is an amazing combination restaurant, bar, sports bar, and game room. The ceiling is at least 30 feet high, and you are surrounded by sides of houses depicting the various styles of architecture that characterize Charleston, Williamsburg, San Francisco, and so on. They serve a very good lunch here for $9.00; dinners are around $15.00. The full menu is at www.redbonealley.com.

The game room features a CD jukebox with more than 1,000 selections. Three pool tables and an air hockey setup are also here. One of the pool tables is L-shaped with eight pockets. Weird. You must be over twenty-one to use the game room, or you must be accompanied by an adult or parent. Call (843) 673–0035.

After lunch, be sure to stop by the **Florence Museum of Art, Science, and History,** if for no other reason than to see the extraordinary work of William Henry Johnson, who painted here in 1940. His childlike but incredibly moving painting *Evening* was painted on rough burlap; his *Christmas Party* and *Rooftops of Denmark* are also worth a peek. Picasso once said it took him twenty years to learn to paint like Rembrandt but all his life to learn to paint like a child. Picasso would have loved Johnson's work. The museum is located at 558 Spruce Street. Open Tuesday through Saturday 10:00 a.m. to 5:00 p.m., Sunday 2:00 to 5:00 p.m. Admission is only $1.00. Call (843) 662–3351. Check out their calendar of events at www .florenceweb.com/museum.

Northeast of Florence, 15 miles away, is **Darlington,** founded in 1785 and the home of the **Darlington 500 motor race,** which is held every Labor Day. You can get the latest NASCAR news at www.darlingtonraceway.com. In the center of the town is a giant mural 100 feet long and 20 feet high painted by Blue Sky, a Columbian artist whose work can be found all over the state. The mural is a rendering of how the old city looked at the turn of the century when a huge oak was the centerpiece of the old town square.

theimportance offat

I once asked an owner of a West Coast salmon packing company why red salmon tasted so good and pink so sorry. His answer was simple and straightforward, "We remove the fat from the pink."
Well, down here we don't remove the fat. My dad once pronounced that "Grease was the secret of the South. When you take it out, all you're doing is ruining it."

I said, "Ruining what?"

And he said, "Everything."

Lee State Park is only 7 miles away on the banks of the Lynches River at 487 Loop Road, Bishopville. The park is open all year and is especially suited for horseback riding. Although they don't provide horses, they do have a stable, a very fine bridle path, and a show ring. Walking-around admission is free; campsites are $11 per night. Call (803) 428–3833. There's more information at www.sciway3.net/outdoors/park-lee. It was here in 1880 that the last duel in the state was fought. The contestants were Col. William S. Shannon of Camden and Col. E. B. C. Cash of Cheraw. They met at Dubose's Bridge, which was in neutral territory. Colonel Shannon was mortally wounded, and his death resulted in a state law against dueling. Even today, South Carolina officials must swear they have not engaged in a duel since January 1, 1881, and that they will not engage in dueling during their term of office.

An even more flamboyant episode in Pee Dee country history was the "Darlington War" of 1894. This was an outbreak caused by Governor B. R. "Pitchfork Ben" Tillman's liquor regulations, particularly his order permitting private homes to be searched without warrant for concealed liquor. In the first skirmish two citizens and one constable were killed, and a number of others were injured. A day later Darlingtonians fired on a train bringing in more constables and began scouring the countryside for other lawmen. Tillman countered by bringing in the militia, but many companies refused to obey and were dishonorably discharged. Among these was the Charleston company, whose members declined to surrender their arms and went on to defend their action in federal court against "one B. R. Tillman, styling himself Governor of South Carolina." Tillman finally collected more docile troops, but by this time the Darlington Guards, a local vigilante group, had restored the peace.

The *Darlington County Historical Commission* is housed in the old city jail at 204 Hewitt Street. Inside are wonderful photographs from more than 100 years ago that portray the history of the town, the growth and decline of the cotton empire, the introduction of the automobile, and other notable events and facts. Also on exhibit are Stephen Foster's original lyrics for "Way Down upon the Swanee River." Originally the river was the Pee Dee, which runs nearby, and you can see where he scratched it out on the manuscript and changed it to Swanee. No one seems to know why. Hours are 9:00 a.m. to 5:00 p.m. No admission charge. Phone (843) 398–4710. There's more at www .darcosc .com/historicalcommission.

The *Darlington Raceway* at 1301 Harry Byrd Parkway, on Route 52, is so big and commanding that there is no way to miss it. Inside the main gate is an interesting museum that features fifteen old racing cars. Each car is equipped with an audio module that tells the history of the car, where and when it ran, and who drove it. Also available is every conceivable piece of memorabilia you can think of, from jackets and caps to postcards and testimonials from famous drivers. Admission is $3.00 for adults; children under twelve are admitted free. Open Monday through Saturday from 9:00 a.m. to 6:00 p.m. Call (843) 395–8499.

If you'd like to see a race, the two big racing weekends are late March and Labor Day, when the big Darlington 500 is run. For those who would just like to see the track, walk down to the white security building at the end of the fence that runs along the front. The guard there will give you permission to climb up the short walk, where you can see the great expanse of curving concrete that is the track. You can also see the stands and the giant billboards. It's a sight you won't soon forget.

Outside Bishopville on Interstate 20 heading west, you'll come to a series of cotton and soybean fields that are as flat as a parking lot. Right in the middle, at Charlene Lane, is a big 6-foot-high red neon sign spelling out simply EAT. It's one of those signs you wonder about. Well, pull off and stop by here. The food is down-home Southern and very good. The new name is **Charlene's Taste of Country,** and they specialize in fried chicken, country-fried steak, great fresh vegetables, and lush desserts. Prices are low, from $6.00 to $9.00. No kidding. Charlene made *Southern Living*'s "Favorite Regional Restaurant" list. That says a great deal. Call (803) 428–2900.

One of the older and prouder Upcountry towns is Winnsboro, the seat of Fairfield County. It was settled in 1755 and named for Col. Richard Winn, Revolutionary officer and early town father. Pennsylvanians and North Carolinians settled here, but along with them came many from the Low Country who were seeking a more healthful climate and broader cotton lands.

Thirty years ago at the corner of Congress and Washington stood a Confederate monument of a lone soldier facing north. After a few of the local "tosspots" banged their Fords and Chevys into it and tried to climb it, it was moved to the park two blocks away. Needless to say, the city fathers saw to it that the soldier still faces north.

roadsidesigns

Near Winnsboro a grocery store sign reads simply DE STO.

The centerpiece of this old town, along with its Confederate soldier, is the town clock and belfry at the corner of Washington and Main. The bell was used as an alarm for fires and curfews and to let the villagers know that fresh meat was available. Tradition has it that there were beaten paths from every direction made by dogs who knew the sound of the bell meant fresh meat for them as well as their masters.

The bell for the clock was made in France, and the story goes that for a long time it had a clear and silvery tone. In 1895, during a fire, it was rung so vigorously it cracked and had to be sent to Philadelphia for repairs. When it was finally returned, the old-timers reported it had lost its silvery tone, and it was doubtful whether or not it was the original bell. In spite of the cracked bell and the shoddy northern repairs, the old clock is the longest continuously running town clock in the United States.

On weekends you might try **Redcoats and Rascals Tavern Restaurant,** 114 East Washington Street (803–635–1331). It's so close to the railroad tracks that the glasses shake when the train comes through. The food is very good, with dinner prices ranging from $8.00 to $17.00. Baking and dessert preparation are all done on the premises. All vegetables are fresh. The Tavern is currently open Thursday through Saturday, closed Sunday through Wednesday. Visit www.redcoatsandrascals.com.

Heading east on Route 34 you'll be through the community of Rockton before you realize it. As a matter of fact, the railroad crossing is the community. On the immediate right you'll see an outdoor museum with no one in attendance. It's the **South Carolina Railroad Museum.** If you're a railroad buff, you can stop and look over the old steam engines and cabooses; they even have a 1930 day coach. Every year a new train or caboose or old engine is added to the collection. And every fall an old-fashioned steam engine cranks up and pulls a few day coach cars up into the mountains for a look at the changing of the leaves. This is a fascinating trip, but since there is no published departure schedule, you will have to phone the Winnsboro Chamber of Commerce at (803) 635–4242 for details. For more about their scheduled runs, visit www.scrm.org/main.asp.

On Route 34 coming into the town of Ridgeway, you might want to stop for a nice Italian meal at the **Olde Town Hall Restaurant,** 140 Palmer Street. This place has retained all the charm of its old-fashioned building where you

Roadside Facts

In small towns there is no law against dogs running loose, and every night you'll see three, four, and five gathering at night under the streetlights and planning their evening. When we lived in Winnsboro, right up the road from Columbia, nine of them wound up living on our porch. I, like a fool, not only bought them food but paid their vet bills and bought them couches and overstuffed chairs from the Salvation Army. One was named Zeke, a direct descendant of one of the somersaulting terriers from the Hunt Brothers Circus, which used to have their winter quarters up the road in Gaffney. At night all nine would line up in full chorus when the trains went through at 2:00 and 4:00 in the morning, and it was the most god-awful beautiful sound I will ever hear.

can now catch an affordable lunch or dinner Monday through Saturday. They have homemade brick-oven pizzas and good manicotti, but I'm especially partial to their stromboli. Check out their full menu at www.oldetownhall.com/menu.htm.

Another fun stop is the ***Ruff and Company Mercantile*** on Highway 21, a general store kind of place that has been in business since 1840. In fact, it's run by the sixth generation of the Ruff family (Dan and John Ruff) who operate it and the "new" store just next door, which was added in 1901. The inventory is just about the same as it has always been—a wide variety of hard-to-find items and general necessities. Here and at their furniture store across the street, you'll see everything from outdoor rockers and porch swings to mattresses and children's toys. This is a real step back in time to the midlands of our grandparents' heyday.

Be sure to take the three-block walking tour of the town and its ***antebellum and Victorian houses.*** There is a beautiful Victorian home constructed by Robert Charleton Thomas in 1906. Note the mounting block in the corner of the front yard. This large block of granite allowed young ladies to step delicately into their awaiting carriages.

The ***Augustus Tally Moore House*** was built in 1899. Mr. Moore's young son was so distressed at seeing a local crippled man that he swore to repair the foot one day. A. T. Moore grew up to become a fine doctor, and he perfected and patented the first artificial hip socket. The first surgery he performed was to repair the foot of the crippled man he had seen as a child.

The ***Charles Wray House*** on Peach Street at the corner of Highway 34 is an enormous and imposing home. Residents say if you look carefully at the attic windows, you may see Charles Wray, who built this home in 1910, staring down the railroad tracks in search of his wife and child, who were killed with him in a tragic train accident.

Revolutionary War Country

Highway 34 east takes you back into Camden. Established in 1732, it is the oldest inland town in the state. For nearly a century Camden was noted for its duels and was the mecca for gentlemen seeking instruction in the code of honor, but this era came to a close in 1880 when dueling was outlawed after the Cash-Shannon duel in Darlington. In 1791, at the corner of Bull and Broad Streets, George Washington addressed the local citizens, but what he said has been lost in the mists of history.

The approach to the town is over the Wateree River Bridge and then through a half-mile of luxurious magnolia trees that seem to stay in bloom all spring and summer. Camden is the home of ***The Carolina Cup Steeple-chase*** in April and ***The Colonial Cup Steeplechase*** in November. If you're here during these times, you can watch the natives drinking champagne as they motor out to the track in their antique cars. Arriving here, they will often spread out an enormous Oriental rug and, after securing the corners with huge vases of cut flowers, arrange a fine silver and crystal picnic in the middle of the infield. Once in a while a group will outdo all the others by showing up in elaborate evening clothes accompanied by a string quartet and, I'm not kidding, a chandelier. If you're interested in attending this event, call the Kershaw County Chamber of Commerce at (803) 432–2525. It's located at 724 South Broad Street. Or visit www.camden-sc.org/things-to-see.php.

The ***Historic Camden Revolutionary War Site,*** located at 200 Broad Street, is a ninety-eight-acre museum open seven days a week, except major holidays. This is the site of the original town of Camden, which was fortified by the British in 1780. Portions of the palisade walls have been rebuilt where they originally stood. The old mansion, built on the war site by Joseph Kershaw, one of the town fathers, was used as British headquarters during the occupation. It has been reconstructed and can be seen on any of the walking tours of the area. There's more at the above Web site if you click on "battle sites."

For a walking tour of Camden, call (803) 432–2525. A quicker, more romantic tour in a horse-drawn carriage can be very colorful. For information, write to the Camden Carriage Company, P.O. Box 1082, Camden 29020, or call them at (803) 425–5737, or check out www.camdencarriage.com. Most of the sixty-odd houses seen on either the walking tour or the carriage tour are private homes and may only be viewed from the street. A few, however, are available for interior tours. Check with the Kershaw County Chamber of Commerce for this information.

For an excellent bed-and-breakfast in downtown Camden, ***The Green-leaf Inn,*** located at 1308 North Broad Street, is at the head of the list. Call (803) 425–1806. Dinner prices in the restaurant range from $15 to $30 with an elaborate dessert followed by coffee, cognac, and hand-rolled cigars out on the veranda. Visit them at www.greenleafinnofcamden.com.

In September 1989 Hurricane Hugo hit not only the Carolina coast but, to everyone's surprise, came barreling inland with winds of more than 110 miles an hour through Sumter, Camden, and all the way up to Charlotte. Camden's big trailer park a few miles to the south of the center of town was devastated; most of the units were completely destroyed. The damage has been repaired, but every September and October people around here begin checking the weather reports and keeping a wary eye on the sky. A calypso song from the Low Country by way of Barbados tells us the months to watch.

June too soon
July stand by
August almost
September remember
October not over

You might need some sustenance after a walking or carriage tour, so head to the **Old South Restaurant** at 402 DeKalb Street (803–713–0009). Although Camden is 100 miles from the coast, the shrimp here is firm and fresh and always available. The plantation chicken, a chicken breast stuffed with oyster and corn-bread dressing and drizzled with a light creamy sauce, is especially good and comes with a little item called Johnny's Stuffed Potato. For dessert, there's chocolate cake and coffee. The total price, including tip, will be about $24, and you'll have a very fine meal. Dinner is served Tuesday through Thursday from 5:30 to 9:00 p.m. and on Friday and Saturday from 5:30 to 10:00 p.m. Lunch is served Tuesday through Saturday from 11:30 a.m. to 3:00 p.m.

One of the best reasons for visiting Camden is to get your bearings and be able to find the town of **Boykin** about 20 miles away. Take Route 521 south and

The Patriot and South Carolina

It wasn't until I saw Mel Gibson in *The Patriot*—an excellent movie that should be required viewing for every South Carolina native—and reread my history that I discovered South Carolina had 245 skirmishes and battles during the Revolutionary War. In fact, most of the war was fought right here. Some of this truly beautiful movie was shot down in the swamps and plantations of the Low Country around Charleston and Beaufort, but most of it was filmed upstate, where much of the war took place. If you're interested in history, the Camden-Winnsboro area 30 miles north of Columbia would be the ideal place to trace most of the action and events. As a matter of fact, at the Historic Camden Revolutionary War Site, located 1.4 miles from Interstate 20 on the outskirts of Camden, they offer guided interactive tours, complete with a videotape made by SC ETV about the Battle of Camden. Only a mile away you can visit the Baron DeKalb Memorial, designed by Robert Mills, who also designed the Washington Monument. DeKalb was the German-born French citizen who became a general in the Continental Army and was mortally wounded during the Battle of Camden. He is buried at a downtown church. The two major battles fought here—the Battle of Camden and the Battle of Hobkirk Hill—resulted in British General Cornwallis's retreat north and his eventual surrender to Washington at Yorktown, Virginia, in October 1781.

Before you visit the old Palmetto State, I'd strongly suggest you see this popular and very fine movie.

turn right at Route 261; drive 4 miles or so. And there you are—that is, if you haven't missed it. It's on the left side of the road, and you have to watch for it.

The millpond and other properties here are owned by the heirs of Lemuel Whitaker Boykin II, six generations from the original 1775 settler, William Boykin II. The entire community, which consists of the General Store, the Broom Place, the Swift Creek Baptist Church, the Mill Pond Restaurant, and the Boykin Mill, is listed on the National Register of Historic Places. Groups are welcome and tours are available.

In the ***Boykin Mill General Store,*** 81 Boykin Mill Road, Rembert, you can get breakfast or a light lunch and then sit out on the porch and watch the road. Almost nothing comes along but an occasional slow-moving dog or an even slower-moving buzzard. The store, with wooden shelves to the high ceiling, sells, among other goods, Boykin's Unsalted Water Ground Grits; stick candy; and raspberry, wild blackberry, and buttered maple syrups. If you want a bologna sandwich, Alice Boykin can take care of it.

Alice or her mother, Alice, or any of the Boykins that are around will be glad to take you on a tour of the 100-year-old mill a few yards away. You'll see grits and meal ground the way they've been ground down here, by water power on hand-dressed millstones, for more than 200 years. Cornmeal, for the record, is finely ground grits. When you see and feel the oil in the fresh grits made here, you'll realize that what you haul down from the supermarket shelves is not only a sin but a true tragedy. The general store is open 9:00 a.m. to 6:00 p.m. Call (803) 424–4731.

Located at 84 Boykin Mill Road, the ***Mill Pond Restaurant,*** one of the very best restaurants in the state, is made up of three buildings, all on the National Register. The building on the left is an elaborate kitchen; the one in the middle is a small dining room with an old-fashioned marble fountain counter serving as a bar; and the one on the right is the main dining room, overlooking the very picturesque millpond, which feeds the mill a couple hundred feet away.

A quick glance at the comments left by guests in the guest book will give you a rough idea of the quality of the food here. From Columbia we hear, "First time—no doggie bag." From Charleston, "Slow but good." From Greenville, "Hard as hell to find but worth it." From Chester, "Ya'll need sweet tea." And finally from Darlington, "Yeeeee-haw!" It's even better than that. Open 5:00 to 10:00 p.m. Tuesday through Saturday. Call (803) 424–0261 or (803) 425–8825 for reservations, which I recommend highly.

Quail hunters of the world should know that Boykin is the home of the Boykin spaniel. Right here is where the Boykin family bred the dog, trained it, and introduced it to the hunting world. For further information on this, you can call the Boykin Spaniel Society at (803) 425–1032. Their Web site is loaded with information at www.boykinspaniel.org.

South Carolina not only leads the nation in poisonous snakes—we have seven kinds—it's also up there on the top ten list of fast-food stores per square mile. If you stay on the main roads you'll see them lined up cheek-by-jowl, and if you're downwind, the grease is so thick you'll have to use your wipers. So stay on the back roads as much as possible—back where they paint ARE YOU READY FOR JESUS? on the rocks and the automobile tires swing in the chinaberry trees.

Route 261 out of Boykin, heading back toward Camden, is a back road. Turn right at Route 521 toward Sumter and 10 or so miles down the road is Rembert, the home of **Lilfred's,** one of the very best European restaurants in the Carolinas and Georgia, located at 11 Main Street. When you're this far off the beaten path, you have to be good to attract the crowd they have been attracting for the past forty-odd years. People come here from everywhere. And they keep coming back. Some of their specialties are rib-eye steak, free-range chicken, oysters Rembert, and onion rings. Prices are $15 to $35 for dinner. It's worth it. It's open 6:00 to 9:30 p.m. Wednesday through Saturday. If you're in the mood to write them, the address is P.O. Box 205, Camden 29020, or call (803) 432–7063.

South of Rembert on Route 521, you'll come to the home of **Shaw Air Force Base** on Highway 378. Many of the attack planes that were used in Desert Storm came from here. When you drive by, you can see them out on the ramps, shooting landings and takeoffs. This restricted base is usually not open to the public, but with advance notice (two weeks minimum) tours can be arranged for groups of twelve or more. Children must be older than thirteen. For more information call (803) 895–2019. The official Web site is www .shaw.af.mil.

Ward's Barbecue, 416 East Liberty Street, Sumter (803–775–2490), is open only on Thursday, Friday, and Saturday from 10:30 a.m. to 7:30 p.m. They are closed Sunday and Monday and cooking is done on Wednesday. Eating barbecue down here is usually done on the weekends, so most barbecue places follow this schedule. At Ward's you can have a barbecue sandwich with a side of coleslaw for $2.75. Soft drinks are available in the vending machine outside. You sit outside on cement chairs at a cement table and watch the trains go by. If you like corn dodgers, which are the same as hush puppies, they are available at $1.50 per dozen. For you barbecue experts out there, Ward's was written up on www.roadfood.com. Be advised, their sauce is ketchup-based.

At the other end of Liberty Street is **Swan Lake Iris Gardens,** one of the most attractive and best-run free city parks in the state. One-hundred-foot-high leaf pine and cypress trees surround the fifty-acre lake. Be sure to take a long look at the cypress knees sticking up from the water—this is how the tree breathes. Out on the lake are six different kinds of swans from all over the world, along with ducks, geese, and herons. May is the big season for the Iris Festival. This is when the six million Japanese irises planted here come into bloom. Azaleas, camellias, and roses also bloom in profusion. An old fire engine is available for kids to climb on, under, and over, which they do by the hour. Call the Sumter Chamber of Commerce at (803) 775–1231 for more information on festival dates.

Due south of Sumter on Highway 6 is *Santee State Park.* This immense tract of land is devoted to fishing, camping, hiking, horseback riding, and golf on the shores of Lake Marion, one of the biggest lakes in the state. Once again, since this is a nonprofit state park, the prices for lodging, golf, camping, fishing, and so on are very reasonable. For information write Santee State Park, 251 State Park Road, Santee 29142, or call (803) 854–2408.

Due west of Santee on Route 301 and then on Route 4, you'll come to the old railroad town of Springfield, where the tracks run right down Main Street. *The Springfield Frog Jump* is the main event here and is held in April every year. Call (803) 258–3152 for exact dates and information. The owner of the winner of the event and the frog itself—you can raise your own frog, or you can buy one from the local kids—are flown out to Calaveras County, California, for the National Jump-Off. The contest here is staged in the middle of the town. After considerable music and ballyhoo about the history and significance of the frog jump, the contestants are asked to step up on the platform and announce where they are from, to whom they are related, and what their frog's name is. Following this the dignitaries lead the contestants and their frogs out to the launching pad. Old-timers in their nineties and children barely out of their mother's arms can and do enter the contest. The frogs' names run

Bombing and Strafing

Here's a slam dunk winner that you will never, ever forget. Shaw Field (Air Force Base), located 20 miles east of Columbia on Route 378, has provided a state-of-the-art showcase like nothing in the entire country. Out on the Poinsett Electronic Combat Range, which features combat planes practicing low-altitude bombing and very low-altitude strafing runs, Shaw Field personnel have erected a set of bleachers for the curious. It's a huge mound with bleachers on top. If you look to the left, you will see the bombing; to the right, the strafing—only 200 yards from where you're sitting. You will also see many of the high-speed planes that fought in Desert Storm. Bring your cameras and ear plugs. This is a real experience, and your kids will love you forever. Since the schedule varies from week to week, call (803) 895–2597 for exact times.

Healing Springs

If you have given up on the medical profession and over-the-counter medication and are suffering from backaches, legaches, and head-, shoulder-, and footaches, there is still hope. It's not only cheap, it's free. All you have to do is get there. And the trip is very, very pleasant. From Columbia take SC 302 south to U.S. Route 178 and turn left. Continue on 178 until you hit SC 3. Turn right on Healing Springs Road—clearly marked. Turn right again on Healing Springs Court. If you see cows in a field, you've gone too far. Back up until you see the stream and twelve spouts that never stop running. This is it!

The hard fact is that every month, thousands of people venture down these very same roads to Healing Springs to wash and drink and carry home the magical elixir. Some carry as many as a hundred one-gallon milk jugs filled with it. A test conducted years ago revealed that city or county water will turn green and slimy in a jar after a few months, but the water from Healing Springs will remain clear. Legend has it that the Cherokee Indians first discovered it and used it until one Nathanial Walker purchased it from a tribal chief for a few bags of grain. Since then the property has gone through six owners until 1944, when the late L. P. Boylston was so moved by the cures that he deeded the land and the springs to God, which allows the springs to remain free to the public. Boylston's deed reads, "I should return to God the most treasured piece of this earth that I have ever owned and possessed."

Many of the faithful will swear they've been cured of everything from lower back pain to heart conditions, and a few will take a blood oath and swear that if people are baptized in the Healing Springs stream or drink from the twelve spouts that never stop running, they won't backslide to their former ways. Hopefully, since Blackville is truly off the beaten path, maybe the *National Enquirer* will leave it alone. As for me, I kept my right hand in the stream for five full minutes, hoping to soften it up at impact on my tee shots and turn my hooks into fades.

While you are in town, you can eat a fine meal at a reasonable price at Miller's Bread Basket, 483 Main Street, Blackville. For more information on the springs and Miller's Bread Basket, call (803) 284–3117. This town is so small that everybody knows everybody.

the gamut from Flash to Captain Marvel to Spiro Agnew to Desert Storm. The method of operation is simple: The frog takes three jumps and the overall length is measured. One enterprising contestant with his eye on the California jump-off introduced his frog to a nonlethal snake at the last second before launching, hoping to scare it into a greater jump. This proved disastrous. The frog froze, relieved himself, and had to be taken away, still staring out into the middle distance; it recovered later and jumped in the consolation trials. The Carolina record is an 18-foot jump, but for the past twenty years most of the Calaveras County, California, winners have been from the West Coast.

Due east about 20 miles from Springfield on Route 4 is Aiken, which is best known for its thoroughbred horses, its polo teams, and the ***Willcox Inn*** at 100 Colleton Avenue (803–648–1898). In the inn's lobby you'll see the two huge stone fireplaces in front of which Franklin Roosevelt and Winston Churchill sat during World War II watching the fire, drinking brandy, and wondering what their next move should be. These boys knew a good thing when they saw it. This inn/spa/retreat is very posh and thoroughly worthwhile.

The ***Aiken County Historical Museum*** at 433 Newberry Street is an enormous 14,000-square-foot house built to display a series of rooms furnished in turn-of-the-twentieth-century style. It also displays agricultural equipment and old firefighting units and has a natural history room. There's a (1808) log cabin, a school classroom (from 1890), and even a 1950s-era drug store. It is open Tuesday through Friday from 9:30 a.m. to 4:30 p.m. and Saturday and Sunday from 2:00 to 5:00 p.m. Admission is free but donations are appreciated. Call (803) 642–2015.

If the ***Palmetto Golf Club,*** located right in the center of Aiken, isn't the oldest course in the country, it's close. Twelve identical rocking chairs sit on the porch overlooking the first tee and eighteenth green—the way they have been sitting since the clubhouse was built in 1902 by none other than Evelyn Nesbit's lover, Stanford White. White was also the man who designed the Shinnecock clubhouse, Madison Square Garden, and Grand Central Station. The

Animal Facts

A mockingbird can and will imitate any sound in the spectrum. It is gray and black with white sergeant stripes on its wings.

Red-tailed hawks will come right down Main Street in any town down here looking for food. If they get hungry enough, they will eat a large pigeon.

Hawks will fly upside down (and have been spotted doing so) so they can grab annoying crows from underneath and kill them. They don't eat them; they just kill them and drop them. Weird, right?

If you see a big hound howling at nothing in particular, wait thirty to forty seconds and you'll hear the train they've picked up with their fine tuning.

Possums—the small dogs that don't bark—are absolutely harmless. Even in Columbia, Charleston, and Greenville, the three big cities down here, they can often be seen at night on the street carrying their litter on their backs.

During the Depression possums were hunted and cooked and even served. I asked my dad how they were eaten. He said, "Fast," and changed the subject.

course itself was remodeled by Alister MacKenzie, the same Scotsman who built the Augusta National, Royal Melbourne, and Cypress Point out in California. Many of the pros stop off at Palmetto for a practice round before they play in the Masters, which is right over the Savannah River a few miles away. In the pro shop is a 1984 photograph of Tom Moore, the pro here, giving Ben Crenshaw some spiritual advice on putting. Crenshaw went on to win the Masters that year, and he's been coming back to see Tom Moore and play Palmetto every year since. He won it again in 1995. Palmetto is a private course, but if you know a pro who knows Tom Moore, there's always a chance you can play here. If you know someone who knows Ben Crenshaw, that would be even better. If you don't golf, this is still a great place to visit. Call (803) 649–2951. There's an interesting story about this club's "exclusivity" at www.tlgolf.com/destinations/9903augusta.html.

A few miles north of Springfield is the town of Salley, the home of the annual *Chitlin Strut,* which is an extravaganza that would be sinful to miss. And what is a chitlin? A Low Country historian is credited with the immortal line, "A chitlin is better discussed than described." Anatomically, they are the intestines of the hog, which normally are used as sausage casings or ground up into lunch meat and hot dogs. Some folks eat them as a dish in themselves. Some even eat a lot of them and actually enjoy them. The long tubelike affair is stretched out and scraped down, turned inside out and scraped again. Then it is stump whipped. Three lengths are braided together, boiled until tender, battered, deep-fat fried, and served. At Salley in late November, as many as five, six, or seven tons of chitlins are served and eaten. One old-time cook said, "Lord, we'd never cook them things here in the summertime. That smell would kill every green thing growing."

During the "boil down" part of the process, no buzzards circle Salley and no jackals stalk the live oaks and the scrub pine. Small dogs whine and cringe, and large ones head for the corn and bean rows to escape the suffocating stench that hangs in the air—impenetrable, insoluble, incredible. An outsider once moaned, "How do ya'll stand it?" The cook answered, "You get so you get used to it. Go sit in the car and turn the air conditioner on. You don't look so good."

During the Strut the town is packed with ten to twenty thousand people all lined up for the hot, greasy fare. They eat and drink beer and lemonade all day and ignore the politicians. Then they hang around for the parade, the beauty pageant, and the high point of the night, the Chitlin Strut Dance Contest. One heavyset dancer I watched one year introduced himself to the crowd as he came shimmy-walking down the center aisle. When he got to the stage, he vaulted over the plastic rhododendron and whipped off an epileptic mountain clog dance that stopped just short of a serious seizure and put the judges in his pocket. Then, swishing his generous hips from side to side, he grinned over his shoulder at the screaming crowd and established one immutable law of the Chitlin Strut. It is not a thin man's dance. It requires bulk, displacement, a stomach, and a rear view of hips, loins, and other choice cuts that a thin man or woman cannot provide. He won the contest hands down and ruled supreme for four straight years.

As with the frog jump, the day of the Strut changes every year, but it's always in late November. Since there are no places to stay in Salley, unless you want to sleep on the ground or in your car, it's best if you get a room in Columbia or over in Aiken. But stay someplace because this is something you'll never, ever forget. Bring your camera. Like the old cook says, "Man, all we have is fun down in here." For information phone (803) 258–3485. There's even an official Web site; it's www.chitlinstrut.com.

Places to Stay in the Fall Line

BENNETTSVILLE
Breeden House Inn
404 East Main Street
(843) 479–3665
www.breedeninn.com

CAMDEN
Greenleaf Inn
1308 North Broad Street
(803) 425–1806
www.greenleafinnofcamden
.com

Places to Eat in the Fall Line

CAMDEN
Old South Restaurant
402 DeKalb Street
(803) 713–0009

REMBERT
Boykin Mill General Store
81 Boykin Mill Road
(803) 424–4731

Lilfred's Restaurant
8425 Main Street
(803) 432–7063

Mill Pond Restaurant
84 Boykin Mill Road
(803) 424–0261

WINNSBORO
Redcoats and Rascals Tavern
114 East Washington Street
(803) 635–1331
www.redcoatsandrascals
.com

Uplands and Columbia

Blue Ridge Foothills

The land north and west of Aiken changes dramatically from low, flat pastureland to lush foothills of the Blue Ridge Mountains and finally to the mountains themselves, which rise to more than 3,500 feet. East of Aiken are the ***J. Strom Thurmond Dam*** and the ***J. Strom Thurmond Lake.*** If this isn't enough Strom Thurmond for you, you can go 20 miles west to Edgefield, where you can see him striding manfully in bronze in the middle of the town square; this is his home. Edgefield is a beautiful town built around a classic courthouse and a small formal square. It has been home to nine South Carolina governors as well as J. Strom Thurmond.

The most famous trial at the courthouse here was the one of Becky Cotton, born in 1780. She killed her first husband by running a mattress needle through his heart; she poisoned her second; and she split the head of her third with an ax. The trial was even more interesting than the murders. While the evidence of her guilt was overwhelming, her beauty was too much for the judge and the jury. Not only was she acquitted, one of the jurymen became her fourth husband.

NORTH CAROLINA
SOUTH CAROLINA

Gaffney

Spartanburg

Rock
Hill

THE PEACH REGION

Greenville

Union

SOUTH CAROLINA

GEORGIA

Anderson

Savannah R.

BLUE RIDGE FOOTHILLS

Newberry

Greenwood

N

THE COLUMBIA
PLATEAU

Columbia

0   30 mi
0   30 km

North Augusta

Later, the author Mason Locke Weems seized on the story for one of his moral pamphlets, "The Devil in Petticoats," or "God's Revenge Against Husband Killing." From his quill we read, ". . . Mrs. Cotton came off clear—nay, more than clear—she came off the conqueror. For as she stood at the bar in tears, with cheeks like rosebuds wet with morning dew and rolling her eyes of sapphires, pleading for pity, their subtle glamour seized with ravishment the admiring bar—the stern features of justice were all relaxed, and both judge and jury hanging forward from their seats breathless, were heard to exclaim, 'Heaven! What a charming creature!'"

West on Route 23 for a couple miles and then up Route 121 for 40 miles through some very fine pastureland, you'll come to Newberry, home of *Newberry College.* Along with the college you'll find whole blocks of historic buildings dating from the 1800s. The college and many of the homes are listed on the National Register of Historic Places. There's more on Newberry College at www.newberry.org.

On Main Street, right in the heart of the old town, is the *Old Newberry Courthouse,* which is now a community hall. The flamboyant relief on the front of the building—an eagle with a palmetto tree in its clutches—symbolizes the federal government's hold on South Carolina during Reconstruction. For further information about the history here and a tour of Newberry College, go

AUTHOR'S FAVORITE PLACES

Cafe and Then Some
Greenville
www.cafeats.com

Chattooga River

Francis Beidler Forest
Harleyville
www.beidlerforest.com

Goatfeathers
2017 Devine Street
Columbia
(803) 256–3325

Riverbanks Zoological Park
420 Rivermount Drive
Columbia
(803) 779–8717
www.riverbanks.org

South Carolina State Museum
301 Gervais Street
Columbia
(803) 898–4921
www.museum.state.sc.us

Trustus Theatre
520 Lady Street
Columbia
(803) 254–9732 www.trustus.org

Old Newberry Courthouse

to the Newberry County Chamber of Commerce at 1109 Main Street, or call (803) 276–4274. Their Web site is www.newberrycounty.org.

Just down the street is Newberry's pride and joy and reason for celebrating—***The Newberry Opera House.*** It was originally built in 1882, but over the years it had deteriorated to the point where it had to be closed. After an extensive renovation, costing more than $4 million, it had a gala opening with the South Carolina Philharmonic performing Beethoven, Bach, and Handel as well as George Gershwin. Camelia Johnson and Kevin Maynor of the Metropolitan Opera were also on stage as well as Hal Holbrook and Dixie Carter. The house has 426 seats and in the past has hosted everyone from Lionel Barrymore to cowboy acts. Nicholas Smith, conductor of the South Carolina Philharmonic, and one of the planners for recent events—which range from opera to "opry"—is very excited about the future. He said, "There's no question, it's going to work; of course it's going to work. There's too much good will, good feelings, good effort for it not to."

A few years ago much of downtown was crumbling and on the verge of falling down. But with the renovated opera house, the centerpiece, the old town has come back to life. Art galleries, antiques shops, and restaurants now line the once-deserted streets and, what is even more important, above the stores people are already moving into apartments. For tickets or more information, write Opera House, Box 357, Newberry 29108, call (803) 276–6264, or visit www.newberryoperahouse.com.

Five minutes from downtown Newberry is the ***Carter and Holmes Nursery*** at 629 Mendenhall Road, where you can see some of the finest orchids in the Southeast on display and for sale. There is no admission charge, and the range and variety of orchids in the greenhouses are nothing less than stunning.

Open from 9:00 a.m. to 5:00 p.m. Monday through Saturday. Call (803) 276–0579. You can even order online at www.carterandholmes.com.

Dining is best done 7 or 8 miles away down Route 17 in Prosperity at the **Back Porch.** I had the barbecued chicken (excellent), green beans, corn and coleslaw, corn bread, and a pitcher of iced tea all for the under $5.00. Then I went next door to the **Back Porch Bakery,** bought a lemon cookie the size of a manhole cover for 45 cents, and then strolled up and down Main Street eating it. Then I went back to the bakery, bought a dozen cookies, a loaf of banana bread, and five slices of red velvet cake and got back on the road. The bakery also sells jams, jellies, and red raspberry preserves. A couple of days later, I learned that people drive 30 and 40 miles to eat lunch and dinner here. I can see why. Open Tuesday through Saturday from 11:00 a.m. to 8:00 p.m. and Sundays from 11:00 a.m. to 2:00 p.m. Closed Mondays. Call (803) 364–3556.

South of Newberry on Route 121, turn right on Route 34 and go about 24 miles to Greenwood, the home of **Park Seed Company,** which is the largest and oldest family-owned mail-order seed company in América. Located at Cokesbury Road and Highway 254, (864) 223–8555, the garden shop and the enormous greenhouses are open from 9:30 a.m. to 6:00 p.m. Monday through Saturday. The best times to visit here are in the spring and during the Festival of Flowers Show in July. More than 70,000 plants are planted in the trial gardens here and can be seen all year-round. Their colorful Web site is www.parkseed.com.

Twelve miles west of Greenwood and perched on a series of small hills is my favorite small town, Abbeville. Centered around a good-sized square and dominated by the tall, thin spire of Trinity Church, the old low-skyline town looks as if it has been here forever. Much work has gone into the preservation of downtown. Everywhere you look, from the hardware store to the drugstore to the poolroom to the Opera House, you realize this is exactly the way the old town was built and it's exactly the way people here are going to make sure it stays. This is a joy to see.

The most prominent building here is the **Belmont Inn,** a Spanish-style hotel built in the 1800s. It originally housed travelers and the performers appearing next door at the **Abbeville Opera House.** The hotel went into a decline in the 1920s, and for a long time it stood unused. Finally, in the 1980s, at the insistence of a very active preservation group here in town, the hotel was renovated and reopened. Today, with its period furniture, elegant rooms, and marvelous restaurant, it once again echoes much of the glory of the old Belmont with the plus that today it has air-conditioning. The dining room, called the Heritage Room, serves continental cuisine. Everything here is excellent. Open for breakfast, lunch, and dinner. Dinner rates run between $15 and

$25; the desserts are exceptional. You might want to write the Belmont Inn at 106 Court Square, Abbeville 29620, or call (864) 459–9625 to find out the performance schedule for the Opera House. Then book a room around your favorite play or musical. Rates for rooms are from $59 and "play packages" start at $159 per night. For more information, visit www.belmontinn.net.

The Abbeville Opera House, next door to the Belmont Inn, doesn't have a bad seat in the place and is absolutely stunning. If you're just passing through town and seeing a show is not possible, just stop and stick your head in. You'll be amazed at the size of the enormous stage and the beautiful construction of the balcony. This is probably one of the best designed theaters in the country, and the Abbevillians take great pride in bringing first-class productions to it year in and year out. The acting and directing talent comes from all over the Southeast, but much of it is from right here in Abbeville County. For reservations and a theater schedule, call the Opera House at (864) 459–2157. Check out www.theabbevilleoperahouse.com.

Beautiful hills, lakes, and horse and cattle country lie northwest of Abbeville as the land rises into the foothills of the Blue Ridge Mountains. But, frankly, there isn't much to do but look at it. The best stop between Abbeville and Clemson is the town of Pendleton. And the best stop here is the bed-and-breakfast, *Liberty Hall Inn,* at 621 South Mechanic Street. This is a 150-year-old family house that has been rebuilt and restored and is now one of the best bed-and-breakfasts in the state. The rooms are large, with high ceilings and heart pine floorboards. They are furnished in antiques. Each room has air-conditioning, a telephone, a television, and a private bath. Local arts and crafts from the town and nearby Clemson University are displayed throughout the inn, and much of that artwork is for sale. Incidentally, the staff all seem to be college students, which gives this unique inn an even nicer touch. Rates are $85 to $89 per night with a continental breakfast. If you're not staying here, you can always eat here. Dinner is served from 5:30 to 8:30 p.m. Thursday through Saturday. Lunch is served from 11:30 a.m. to 2:00 p.m. Tuesday through Friday. Prices are $15 to $25.

footballmania (clemsontigers)

Coon Williams, a local scribe, once said, "Some anthropologists maintain that Clemson tailgating is a cultural event comparable to the 'Chitlin Strut' and the 'Springfield Frog Jump.' But I say there is nothing out there on the boards as outrageous as 80,000 Clemson fans shrink-wrapped in orange (the school color) eating and drinking, listening to taped highlights of the '81 season (the year they won the National Championship), and their 'Tiger Rag' auto horns blaring and standing in line for the Port-O-Johns—and that's why I love them." Here ends the chronicle.

Tigers versus Gamecocks

You'd need a phone-book-thick volume and a ten-hour miniseries to even touch the lore, the action, and the downright insanity of college football down here. First of all, the number one game—and it's the day the state shuts down—is between the Clemson Tigers and the University of South Carolina Gamecocks—a game that goes back to the beginning of time. Tickets are impossible to get. Many are passed on in wills, others are divided up during divorces and right over the graves at funerals, while others are bought on the open market for the price you'd pay for a good used car.

Most people don't even try to get tickets. Some arrive at Clemson Stadium and park their Winnebago near the walls, open their chaise lounges, plug in their TV sets, and turn on the radio. Radio announcers are not only much better down here than TV announcers, they know the players and their families and, if pushed, can come up with exactly where they live and the name of their dogs. The spokesman for one group who had gathered at Clemson put everything in perspective. "Friend, what if we got four sets of tickets—which we won't anyhow—but say we did just for argument's sake. First of all we'd have to split up, and we don't want to do that. We've been together for twelve years now. This way we stay together, we don't have to fight the crowd, we can drink all the beer we want, and the john's right here. Hell, all our friends know we're here, and they all come by for some barbecue and pimento cheese. And I'll tell you something else. When the Tigers score and that noise goes up and the old stadium starts rocking, I wouldn't trade this spot for eight box seats with the Board of Trustees."

The wine list is impressive, and other spirits are, of course, available. Call (864) 646-7500. Don't try to stay here during the football season—it's booked solid. There's more information at www.bbonline.com/sc/liberty.

While you're in the Pendleton area, you're too close to Clemson not to drive through and look over the *Clemson University* campus, which features great redbrick buildings, rolling hills, and beautiful trees. The school is famous for textile engineering, architecture, and the liberal arts, and many of its graduates are employed by the big international firms in Greenville and Spartanburg a few miles away. Clemson is also famous for its football, basketball, soccer, and baseball teams. There's more on Clemson at www.clemson.edu.

As a matter of fact you'll need some luck if you want to see a football game. Despite the fact that the stadium seats 80,000, seats are sold out years in advance. But for the dedicated there is a way. Don't go to the stadium; go to the *Esso Club* and just stand around—something will happen. It could be a fight, someone might pass out, or die . . . as I said, something. But hang around long enough, and you'll get a ticket. Read more lore about this place at www.theessoclub.com.

Thirty miles northeast of Pendleton is the tiny crossroads town of Salem. The best way here is up Route 11, but you'll have to watch for the signs. A mile out of town on a high-rising hill—you are now in the high foothills of the Blue Ridge Mountains—is the **Sunrise Farm Bed and Breakfast Inn** at 325 Sunrise Drive. The guest rooms are nicely appointed with period antiques, thick comforters, and family heirlooms. Large windows provide wonderful views of the mountains. This area is famous for hiking and rafting on the nearby Chattooga River. Rates run from $95 to $190 per night, including breakfast. For reservations and further information, call (864) 944–0121. Their Web site is www.bbonline.com/sc/sunrisefarm.

On the shores of Lake Jocassee, which many consider the most beautiful lake in the state, is **Devils Fork State Park** at 161 Holcombe Circle, Salem. Built in cooperation with Duke Power Company, it is managed by the Division of State Parks. Twenty luxurious mountain villas, fifty-nine campsites, swimming facilities, boat ramps, and picnic areas are available. Day admission is only $2.00. For more information and reservations, call (864) 944–2639 or see www.southcarolinaparks.com.

From Salem a nice trip would be northeast to Sassafras Mountain, which is 3,560 feet and the highest point in South Carolina. This is a wild and beautiful part of the state, and some of the vistas out over the mountains and valleys look a great deal like Scotland. Driving here at night you'll be amazed how bright the stars are. You'll also be surprised by how few lights you see.

The Greenville Area

Many small cities boast of a renaissance in their downtown areas, but few have delivered on the claim like Greenville. It could be her sister-city relationship with Bergamo, Italy, that made the city planners take the concept as seriously as they have, but more than ten years of effort have made a difference that few could have imagined. You can get a nice overview of Greenville at www .greenville.com.

The new downtown is a showpiece anchored by the restored **Westin Poinsett Hotel**, with restaurants, coffee shops, sidewalk cafes, and lots of things to do and places to see—all in walking distance of one another. Feeling bookish? Or maybe you want to see an outstanding art exhibition? How about taking in a play? You can find what you want all in an area of two city blocks at **Heritage Green**, home to the county library, the Greenville Little Theatre, and the **Greenville Museum of Art**. The Greenville County Library is bright and spacious (designers have made exceptional use of glass throughout) and includes a coffee shop; a large video, books-on-tape, and CD center;

and a non-circulating research collection of South Carolina history and culture. Next door to the library, the Little Theatre features regular first-rate productions (Joanne Woodward is an alumna, after all) and just one door from the theater is the Greenville Museum of Art, for years the home of the Wyeth Collection and still showing pieces by many nationally and world-renowned artists. If you happen to be a fan of Andrew Wyeth's work, you'll be very impressed with this museum's collection. Emphasizing his watercolor portraits and landscapes, the Wyeth collection represents every phase of the artist's storied career. Wyeth himself called it "the very best collection of my watercolors in any public museum in this country." But there's also a nice collection of Impressionist art here, and they always have a timely and uplifting traveling exhibit up and ready to enjoy. This is a "hidden" gem you don't want to miss. You can write them at 420 College Street, Greenville, 29601, or call (864) 271–7570. There's much more on the Greenville Museum of Art at www.gmoa.org.

A block away is the local favorite, *Cafe and Then Some.* One block up and a right turn (still walking) and you are on Main Street, at the hub of the downtown renewal. The other anchor of the area, *The Hyatt Regency,* invites you into a glass atrium, with restaurant and bar, the perfect start to an evening. Moving down Main Street, you will find eateries, bistros, tobacco and clothing stores, and gift shops. As you walk through *Bergamo Square,* you will find that many of the restored buildings are home to new residents of the downtown area, remodeled walk-up flats that are also just a walk away from the office. During the spring and summer months, as well as early fall, live bands give free concerts in the square every Thursday, and downtown festivals celebrating almost any occasion regularly turn the area into the upstate's largest block party.

Your next stop, only three blocks down from the square on Main Street, is *The Peace Center,* a gem of a concert hall that was built in 1989 and named after one of its primary benefactors. The center is a regular draw for touring Broadway musicals, concerts, and solo artists. It was also the site in 2004 for one of the nationally televised Democratic primary presidential debates; the moderator, NBC's Tom Brokaw, was so impressed, the evening news for that night was anchored from the center. The Peace Center is also part of a pavilion that includes restaurants, banquet facilities, and an open-air forum for speakers, artists, and social functions. Check out www.peacecenter.org.

Baseball fans take note: The city is home to the Class A minor league baseball team (and Boston Red Sox affiliate) Greenville Drive. The team's home stadium is located just off of West Main, and provides ample parking for fans in county office spaces only two blocks away. For those not up for a walk, trams run every ten minutes to deliver you to the front gate of the stadium. If you want to leave early, stop for dinner at the **Brick Street Café** and order a bowl of gumbo, one of the daily specials, and top it off with a generous piece of carrot or pineapple cake and a cup of cinnamon coffee (315 Augusta Street; 864–421–0111). Check them out at www.brickstreetcafe.com.

Even if you have never been to West End Field for a game, you might feel a sense of déjà vu as you enter the stadium. No surprise there; the Drive is a part of the Boston Red Sox organization and the ballpark is a remarkable replica of the field in Boston, down to Greenville's own version of the fabled Green Monster in left field.

Just across from the front gate is the **Shoeless Joe Jackson Museum,** housed in the home of the baseball great claimed by both Pickens County (where he was born) and Greenville (where he played textile league baseball and spent his later years).

Ticket prices at the stadium, as well as prices for the hot dogs, barbecue, popcorn, and beer, are also a welcome throwback to the days when a family of four or a couple wanting to spend a night watching America's pastime could do it all without breaking the bank.

The Haywood Road area is the heart of what the locals call the Eastside—malls, restaurants, bookstores, shopping, all minutes from four hotels just off Interstate 385. In the mood for steaks, drinks, and good company? Try **John Paul's Armadillo Oil Company Inc.,** a cross between a tavern and a hunting lodge at 637 Congaree Road (864–288–8607), for good, casual dining at reasonable prices ($15 to $20 per person, with an appetizer). If you lived in the upstate or across the line in Charlotte during the early 1960s, you might listen closely when you meet your host, owner and operator John Paul, usually there greeting friends, regulars, and newcomers, all with the same warm handshake and raspy voice. The sound of that voice should be familiar, and suddenly you just might hear music, like maybe the Temptations, the Tams, or the Four Tops. In the golden '60s, you knew the voice of John Paul as the nighttime disc jockey on WAYS in Charlotte, Long John Silver (he still wears the familiar black eye patch). He was the one who kept you posted with his Super Wonder Dog Blue on the latest in pop music and the results just in from folks parked out at the airport watching the submarine races. John Paul's Web site is www.johnpauls.com.

If you're looking for something different, try the buffalo steak at **Saskatoon Steaks, Fish and Wildgame,** 477 Haywood Road (864–297–7244), or something hot and bubbly at ***The Melting Pot,*** a fondue restaurant, 475 Haywood Road (864–297–5035), or hot and spicy at ***Chili's Grill and Bar,*** 490 Haywood Road (864–281–0547). Want fine dining? Try ***Stax's Peppermill,*** 30 Orchard Park Road (864–288–9320), which offers intimate dining with a piano bar, at approximately $30 to $50 and up, per person, with wine, or maybe breakfast at ***Stax's Omega,*** known for Greek omelettes made with feta cheese and spinach, Greek toast, and home-fried potatoes, with coffee for under $10.

At the end of the evening, you may just want to read the paper and enjoy a cup of coffee and something sweet. Drop by Barnes & Noble Bookstore at 735 Haywood Road (864–458–9113), or Books-a-Million at 265 Laurens Road (864–281–1301). Yes, I know, they are national chains, but the people are local, the food and coffee really good, and although you're in a strange city, the feeling is one of a large coffeehouse with a lot of great books and magazines, and friends waiting to be introduced. All you have to do is start the conversation by mentioning something interesting you've read lately.

If you're staying anywhere on the Eastside off Interstate 85 (maybe going north to Charlotte or south to "Hotlanta"), then the Pelham Road area may offer some easy dining choices, once you decide which of the many is for you. Most are chains, and most are located off East Beacon Road (or East Beacon Drive, coming the other way), the Eastside's restaurant row. The food is good at any of them.

Want Italian? Stop in at ***Tony Roma's,*** 103 East Beacon Drive (864–627–1339), or ***Romano's Macaroni Grill,*** 105 East Beacon Drive (864–675–6676). For seafood, there's ***Joe's Crab Shack***, 102 East Beacon Drive (864–987–0009); for Mexican, there's ***On the Border Mexican Grill and Cantina,*** 74 Beacon Drive (864–234–0112); and for a little bit of everything fixed just right, try ***California Dreaming,*** 40 Beacon Drive (864–234–9000). All of these offer very good meals at prices generally in a range of $15 to $20 per person, within a two-minute drive from the Greenville-Spartanburg Airport Marriott Hotel and within walking distance of each other.

The crown jewel of restaurant row is ***Chop House 47,*** 36 Beacon Drive (864–286–8700), an excellent choice for fine dining and drinks. The service is terrific, and you might dress up a bit for the evening, a dining experience worth the price ($50 and up per person, with wine or cocktails), if you want to do it right. For more on Greenville's Restaurant Row, visit www.greater greenville.com.

South Carolina is all about barbecue, a state where the Uplands claim a ketchup base is the only way to go, the Midlands claim a mustard base is the only way, and the Low Country claims a vinegar base is . . . well, you get the idea. *Little Pigs Bar-B-Q* offers chopped barbecue prepared daily, regular and jumbo sandwiches and plates, with coleslaw, beans, and fries on the side. You can get a sandwich for $2.79, a plate for $4.59, and feed the family with a chopped half pound for $7.59. Located on 291 Bypass, at Lake Forest Shopping Center, across from Bob Jones University; (864) 268–2020.

You wanna play pool or billiards? If the latter, spend a coupla grand and get your own table, but if it's pool you want, *The Corner Pocket* is the place. It has been renovated and is more upscale than when a former governor was a teenager first learning the hustle (our kind, not that disco stuff), but it is still the place downtown where you can rack 'em and play by the hour. The bar is friendly, and the menu has some good appetizers and lunch plates. Reasonably priced, especially if you talked that kid who just walked through the door into a game of eight ball, loser pays. Corner Pocket Tavern and Oyster Bar is at 21 East Coffee Street; (864) 242–3432. There's more at www.cornerpocket tavern.com.

Beano Brothers Coffee and Cafe is definitely not on the beaten path, at least not for those looking for a cup of coffee and something to eat during the morning rush. But it is located without fanfare in the much-traveled Pelham Road area of Greenville. It offers good coffee and a gathering spot for mornings and afternoons during the week, and lunch Monday through Saturday. Try the blueberry or cranberry bread weekdays with a cup of Beano Blend for breakfast and for lunch a Papa's Polo or Mama's Seta followed by a cappuccino grande. Lunch is under $10. It's at 4 Independence Pointe, behind the Observatory (864–675–0303); takeout available.

"The best steaks around downtown." A lot of native Greenvillians will tell you that's what's waiting at *Charlie's Steak House,* a Greenville touchstone for great food in a casual, friendly atmosphere. Your steak is cooked to order with baked or fried potatoes, bread, and a salad. You'll find yourself in a true old-fashioned steakhouse when you step from the curb through the door at 18 East Coffee Street (864–232–9541). Dinner with a drink will run around $20. Visit www.charliessteakhousegreenville.com.

Trio Brick Oven Cafe (864–467–1000) is a downtown favorite for lunch or dinner, located at 22 North Main Street, the corner of Main and Coffee. The service is good, the menu distinctive with lots of Italian dishes and a sampling from the South to choose from. Generous servings of the penne goat pasta or the baked chicken (with skin or skinless) with cooked potatoes will leave you ready for a walk through the downtown sights. Lunch or dinner with a glass of wine will run about $10 to $15 per person.

Greenville has some excellent coffee houses, and not just the standard franchise variety. *Coffee Underground* is at 1 East Coffee Street. This is not just another Mickey Ds. Comfortable sofas and chairs are arranged for relaxed conversation, giving you time to enjoy your cup with a piece of strawberry cake, cheesecake, or any number of other good choices. Or go ahead and just order a decaf—they'll know you're not a regular, but they'll still let you drink it at your pace and enjoy the movie (yep, they have them free more than occasionally). Call (864) 298–0494.

Nick and Iris Tassopoulos have a good thing going. They know it and so does anybody who eats at *Never on Sunday Greek Restaurant,* located at 210 East Coffee Street in downtown Greenville. Lunch or dinner, the food is always excellent, the service outstanding (Iris serves while Nick mans the kitchen) and there is always something on the menu that is truly Greek and truly great. The two-room dining area is cozy and casual, decorated with a touch of the old country and photos of friends, old and new. They can handle appetites from two to ten at one sitting, with a menu that goes from the standard favorite, moussaka, to other more special dishes, to be accompanied by a glass of wine or the best iced tea in the upstate (Iris has a secret to preparing it—ask and she might tell you, if she decides you're a friend). Be sure and order the bakhlava for dessert, but you have to eat it with the fingers (Iris can tell if you are going to be a regular or just passing through by this little test). Lunch or dinner for around $10 to $15 per person; call (864) 232–2252.

Travinia Italian Kitchen is one of the new restaurants in the area, opening in 2003 at 1625 Woodruff Road (864–458–8188). It is already one of the best Italian restaurants in the greater Greenville area with a menu that has familiar dishes like pasta (pasta mia nona, sausage and peppers rustica, and homestyle canneloni), as well as salads that everybody knows (a great Caesar) or some that you have to try (belgian endive and Granny Smith apple salad). The portions are generous, and a meal that includes any of these dishes with a glass of wine costs about $20. The bar is a good one, the atmosphere includes lots of Sinatra, Tony Bennett, and other favorites, easy lighting, and comfortable booths. Coming from Columbia and other places south, take the Woodruff Road exit off I–385, turn right onto Woodruff Road, drive approximately 2 miles, and you are there, on the left. Check out www.travinia.com. Even the photos are delicious.

City Range Steak House Grill is the best thing for appetites near Haywood Mall. And there is a lot going on in either direction when you take the Haywood Road exit from I–385. The area has many good restaurants, but City Range's southwestern decor, view-through fireplace, two dining areas, and intimate bar make it something special. Add to this the fine service and a menu that includes such varied specialties as honey pecan and gorgonzola salad, butter crumb trout, herb-crusted rib eye, or lamb loin chops. Dinner and a drink will be around $30 to $35 per person. Located at 615 Haywood Road (864-286–9018). Their Web site is www.cityrange.com.

If you're looking for good music, dancing, and some company, there is all of that and more at the **Blind Horse Saloon,** a popular watering hole that features new talents on the rise in country music, 1025 Lowndes Hill Road; (864-233–1381). In the downtown area there is **The Handlebar,** a club featuring something for almost everyone's choice of music; a mix of nationally recognized musicians and regional and local talent, folk music balladeers, and hard-rocking Grammy winners (304 Stone Avenue; 864–233–6173).

There are two unique experiences for dining just off Wade Hampton Boulevard. If you want outstanding food with an intimate atmosphere, try **Justin's Steakhouse,** named by owners Bernie and Candy Kavo for their son. A picture of him, number six walking to the plate in his little league uniform, is one of many photos of sports legends that adorn the walls of a restaurant that somehow manages to balance a feeling of family atmosphere with upscale dining. The menu has truly exceptional fare waiting for you, including favorites such as the osso bucco, or perhaps the bone-in rib eye, made using only Black Angus beef, as with all the steaks on the menu. However Justin's also offers Kobe beef for three of its cuts: the filet, strip, and rib eye. For an appetizer, try the grilled brie or the smoked mozzarella, but whatever you do, save room for dessert. The crème brûlée or the white chocolate croissant pudding with crème anglaise will be worth easing the car seat back a notch for the ride home (40 Rushmore Drive; 864–322–2626; another Justin's is located in Greer at 109 Trade Street; 864-801-8884). For more information (and information on two other locations in Simpson and Spartanburg), see www.justinssteakhouse.com.

A bit further out, still just off Wade Hampton Boulevard as you head toward Greet, a short detour will bring you to the **English Country Tea Rooms,** a small and intimate restaurant that offers traditional specialties from across the pond; everything from tea and crumpets, to pasties, beef or lamb pies, fish and chips, or puddings—their kind, not ours, which is another course not just a dessert (6 East Lee Road, Taylors; 864–322–5831).

Continuing your drive all the way out Wade Hampton Boulevard will bring you to another city renovation and revival that has proven that, just like neckties and scarves, sometimes the old becomes new again. The city of Greer has worked to restore the downtown area as well as create a civic spirit, which is a bit like sharing a block party with the neighborhood. Which means that during the spring, summer, and fall months, on any calendared holiday (and some apparently created just because the weather permitted), there are concerts, shows, or art exhibits in the downtown area, all within a short walk of a few blocks from one another. In the fall of 2006, the city held its first Oktoberfest. If you want to do a little shopping, the remodeled Old Greer Railway Station serves up some nice possibilities, named collectively and appropriately enough, *The Shops at the Old Greer Station.* A luncheon at the *Southern Thyme Café* (219 Trade Street; 864–801–9551) or a cup of java at, well, *Hot Java Coffee House* (117 East Poinsett Street; 864–334–0115) is a sample of the good life made simple.

At the junction of Highway 14 and Highway 11 (11250 New Cut Road), you can find a secret, one they know about in a small part of four counties and two states. They call it the *Links O' Tryon,* a semiprivate club that features an eighteen-hole golf course, an Olympic-size swimming pool (club membership required), and tennis courts. The Links course is set near the foothills of the upstate—eighteen challenging holes tailored for the shot maker by Tom Jackson, a course architect who started his career under Robert Trent Jones. The clubhouse has a restaurant open to the public that offers lunch including Reuben, crab cake, and Philly steak sandwiches, as well as luncheon and dinner specials and a regular Sunday brunch menu. Lunch will run $5.00 to $10.00, brunch around $15.00, and dinner $20.00 to $30.00 per person; call (864) 468–5099, Greenville; (864) 472–6723, Spartanburg; or (888) 525–4657. Visit www.linksotryon.com for more information.

The upstate of South Carolina is growing and every year welcomes new and significant additions to its already strong Hispanic communities. One of the nice benefits from this are some excellent restaurants, including *El Chile Rojo,* located in the center of Landrum and just across the line in Tryon, North Carolina. The service is excellent, the staff friendly, and the menu offers a little of everything that you might be familiar with, plus a few dishes that you need to find out about. A meal with tea or coffee runs under $10. Two locations, 209 East Rutherford, Landrum (864–457–5977), and 334 South Trade Street, Tryon, NC (828–859–6858); catering at (803) 783–2470.

The *Peddler Steak House* is a cut above. Reservations are only for parties of ten or more, but a well-arranged plan for seating and serving, along with a nostalgia-filled bar and seating room, usually makes the wait quick and comfortable. In cold weather, wood fires are kept burning in original stone fireplaces, pleasant reminders that you are dining in a renovated stone and wood farmhouse. The salad bar is excellent, and starts you off until the meat cutter makes his way to your table to offer the cut of steak you choose. Although a menu is posted, most diners prefer the steaks, which bring them back time and time again; dinner with a cocktail will run about $30 to $40 a person. A bargain buy if you go often is a Peddler Card, purchased annually for ten visits. It allows you to purchase an entree and enjoy another one free for your guest. Find it at 2000 Poinsett Highway (864–235–7192) in Greenville.

So maybe you're headed down Highway 11 and you come to the cross-roads again, the junction with Highway 14. This time, you want to go right, do a little exploring to the north. Head up Highway 14 just a few miles and you're in Landrum, at another junction, where Highway 14 becomes West Rutherford Street and Highway 176 becomes Howard Street. Across the rail tracks you will find another successful revamping of a downtown, staring at *The Hare & Hound,* a small tavern that local folks will tell you used to be Wilson's Five and Dime, where candy and gum were sold by the piece from large barrels. The address is 101 East Rutherford Street, and there's more at www.thehareandhound.com.

After checking out the shops in Landrum, drive a few miles farther north on Highway 176 and across the state line to a special treasure: Tryon, North Carolina. As you enter Tryon you pass shops and antique stores *(The Old Mill Flea Market)* along the way to the downtown square, 8 to 10 blocks that you can browse through at your leisure (free two-hour parking). At *The Shops of Tryon,* a building renovation turned walk-in mall, start at *Simple Simon's Sweets and Savories,* offering ice cream, pastries, and very good coffee to take with you on your stroll. Be sure to step into the framing and art galleries on both sides of Trade Street, the antiques and bookstores, *Buck's Pizza, Trade Street Gallery Coffee House,* and maybe finish with a beer or glass of wine at *Preston's Pub & Grill* with the locals. If you stay until evening, you can take in a movie. Man, oh man, can you take in a movie.

The *Tryon Theatre* is an original, a landmark, a for-real movie house that dates back to the days of first-run epics like *Ben Hur* and *Spartacus,* to the times when Doris Day comedies and Alfred Hitchcock suspense thrillers ruled, to the days of musicals and Saturday matinees. The owner and manager, Barry Flood, has preserved a time capsule for film buffs and updated it just enough for the fans of a new era. In spring 2004, he put in new (but still conventional, 1950s-style) seats. The Tryon Film Society meets at the theater to vote on selections the second and fourth Monday and Tuesday of each month; membership is $12.00 per year and provides a $1.00 discount on tickets for each show. Feature presentations are at 8:00 p.m. Wednesday through Saturday, $5.00 per person, and a matinee on Sunday at 3:00 p.m. for $4.00. Popcorn and soft drinks come in two sizes, small ($2.00) and large ($3.00), with more generous servings than other theaters. If you like, sit in the balcony and choose from several good beers they offer, or maybe a glass of wine. Want coffee? They've got coffee, from Little River Roasting Company in Spartanburg. Try to put this in perspective, folks. Between the Outer Banks of North Carolina and just about any part of the Gulf Coast, there are two places to find a theater this great—one is in Tryon, and the other is somewhere else. Call (828) 859–6811 or visit www.tryontheatre.com.

So you've finished your walk through town, had a treat or a beer, picked up something to take home, seen a good movie . . . what next? By now you may want to retire here (that's just what Perry Como did, 7 miles up the road in Saluda)—or at least retire for the night. As Tony Bennett might say, the best is yet to come.

You can stay at **The Tryon Bed & Breakfast** or the **Mimosa Inn,** both reasonably priced and comfortable, or if you decide to make it a long week-end, heavy on the romance in style, call ahead for reservations at **The Pine Crest Inn,** up New Market Road from Trade Street, left on Pine Crest Lane. The Pine Crest just may be the finest little hotel of its kind in the Carolinas, a triple-A, four-diamond award winner arranged as a compound of twelve cottages and a main lodge with thirty-five rooms. The main building was constructed in 1906, then bought by horseman Carter Brown, who converted it into an inn and owned it until it was bought by the current owners, one of whom is Carl Caudle, who also acts as host and general manager, along with Deborah and Barney Dubois.

The main lodge is informal and cozy, decorated in warm colors, and furnished with a mix of antique wood and glass curio cupboards, sofas, and tables arranged on hardwood floors covered with fine rugs—ideal places for drinks and conversation in front of two fireplaces. One of the rooms also serves as a bar and small library for reading while you wait for the main event of the evening dinner in the inn's restaurant. The restaurant is all about fine dining, gourmet southern foothills cuisine with a bit of French and Italian as well. Crab cakes made only with fresh lump crabmeat from North or South Carolina and calamari are just two of the appetizers, followed by menu regulars, such as lamb chops served with warm goat cheese and red pepper jelly and the filet mignon, only from Black Angus beef, served with a rotation of sauces to keep a regular favorite from becoming routine. Dessert is prepared by the pastry and bread chef, a graduate of the Cordon Bleu, and the crème brûlée is only one of the two house specialties. The wine cellar has more than 900 labels. Dinner for two runs $100 to $150 per person, more with wine (some selections are $500 per bottle).

Reservations for the inn are recommended. During most months, a week ahead is fine to assure availability of a room, suite, or cottage. Spring, summer, and fall are all busy seasons, with January, February, and March generally slower. Rooms are at a premium during the week of the **Block House Steeplechase,** Tryon's annual horse race held in mid-April, unless you make reservations at least one month ahead. Check (800) 633–3001, (828) 859–9135, or www.pinecrestinn.com for rates, reservations, and more information about rooms, cottages, and availability.

Take Highway 11 to the Cleveland Junction with Highway 276, turn right and keep going, past the little waterfall on the right where the vendor has her stand selling apples, cider, and coffee. Then bear left at the fork in the road ahead, still on Highway 11, and continue on through the rolling, wooded hills of Pickens County for about 12 miles, to the wooden sign ahead on the right that announces: TABLE ROCK STATE PARK. The lake is on the left all the way up the winding road to the lodge. Table Rock Lodge was built by the Civilian Conservation Corps as part of FDR's New Deal, and was one of the many construction projects of the Corps from 1933 through 1942. The lodge has in the past been a favorite dining spot for many in Greenville and Pickens Counties, but closed in March 2004 for remodeling. Newly restored to its former glory, the lodge is no longer a restaurant but a venue for private events (like weddings and parties) and occasional musical performances. You oughta hear their bluegrass pickin'. Call (864) 878–9813 for scheduling.

You like fresh seafood but you can find it only on the coast, right? Not so. **The Flounder** is a Spartanburg mainstay, a family seafood restaurant along the lines of the old-time fish camp, complete with wooden booths, aluminum trays, and a basic menu that is reasonably priced. The flounder fillet and oyster stew are among the favorites (dinner includes coleslaw, hush puppies, french fries, and tea, all for under $10), served up by a second and third generation of owners and operators from 4:00 until 9:00 p.m., Wednesday through Saturday. There is usually a line by 5:00 p.m. but fine service and a large dining area help move it quickly. On I–85 north from Greenville, exit numbers have changed with the interstate alterations following the opening of the giant BMW plant in the Midlands area. At the I–85 fork (Charlotte or Spartanburg), take the Spartanburg lane, then the next exit to the stop sign; turn left and then right just after the overpass, and follow the frontage road until you are there, on Pottery Road (864–576–3165).

The Peach Region

Until twenty years ago the Midlands area was largely supported by textile mills, cotton, soybeans, tobacco, and a huge peach crop. Now we see a growing industrial revolution, the centerpiece of which is the enormous BMW plant.

Spartanburg, with an elevation of about 900 feet, is in the foothills of the Blue Ridge Mountains. The county and the city get their name from the Spartan Regiment, a body of South Carolina militia that was formed in this area and served with distinction during the Revolution. Its most noteworthy engagement was at Cowpens, in what was one of the decisive battles of the war.

Today Spartanburg is a surprisingly cosmopolitan city. It has even taken on an international quality. A good example of this change is the very fine

Peach water tower

Gerbard's Cafe at 1200 East Main Street, right on the town square. They feature a menu of German and Austrian entrees as well as pastas, duck, rack of lamb, and pepper steak. Prices are from $15 to $28. Open for dinner Monday through Saturday. Call (864) 591–1920.

Seven blocks away on Church Street, with a high hilltop setting of sixty-five acres or so, are the beautiful old, redbrick buildings of ***Wofford College,*** founded in 1850 and governed by the Methodist Church of South Carolina. The school is internationally known for its program in the liberal arts, especially in English and history. On the campus is a simple granite monument over the graves of Dr. Benjamin Wofford, the founder, and his wife, Anna Todd. The monument bears the same Latin inscription as the grave of Sir Christopher Wren, translated as IF YOU WOULD SEE THIS MONUMENT, LOOK ABOUT YOU. There's much more about Wofford at www.wofford.edu.

As you drive northwest from Spartanburg on I–85, the kids will spot the big peach first. It's an enormous one-million-gallon water tower painted like a ripe peach, and it's meant to tell you that you're getting close to Gaffney, the home of the ***Gaffney Peach Festival.*** This is peach country—as a matter of cold fact, Spartanburg and Cherokee Counties produce more peaches than all of Georgia. Gaffney, a town of 13,600, is the home of the peach festival, which takes place the first week of July and attracts as many as 300,000 people. For more information, visit www.scpeachfestival.org. Gaffney is also the home of ***Limestone College,*** the state's oldest institution of higher education for women. See more on Limestone at www.limestone.edu. Here, you'll also find at least a dozen National Register homes that date back to the early 1800s.

Here's a little background on Gaffney. Back in 1835 promoters took over the town and ballyhooed it as the South's Saratoga. This was the heyday of therapeutic mineral treatment, and plantation owners from Charleston and the Low Country, plagued every summer by malaria, flocked here to drink the water, gamble in the casino, and visit the racetrack. Gaffney also became famous for its jousting tournaments, cockfights, and gander pullings (which is the fine but mercifully lost art of snatching off the head of a plucked and greased goose while riding at a hard gallop).

After this medicine-show enterprise failed, Gaffney evolved into a thriving textile mill center until the mill closings of the last thirty or so years. Today, four mills are still here, employing about 2,000 workers, and the Nestlé Frozen Food Company and Timken Roller Bearing Company also operate here, but downtown Gaffney has been neglected and allowed to go to seed. One can hope that one day they will follow Greenville's lead and renovate a few of the old buildings, plant some trees, and bring the old town back to life, but in the meantime this is still a good stopover because you can see the beautiful buildings of limestone and the old homes.

If you want to find the perfect place to get an idea of how an old mill town must have felt not too many years ago, go to **Harold's Restaurant** in the heart of downtown Gaffney. It has a four-table poolroom and bar next door, and it does a thriving lunch and short-order business, with prices right out of the 1960s. A chicken salad sandwich, which is very good, is only $1.00; a pint of coleslaw is only $1.50. During the peach festival people line up for the take-out specials—a pint of chicken salad at $3.50, a gallon of chili for $18.00. Reservations aren't needed, but if you want to order over the phone and then pick it up, call (864) 489–9153. The new owner, Tony Lipscomb, is very young and very personable and will be glad to tell you about Gaffney and the peach festival. You can't miss Harold's at 602 North Limehouse Street.

Back on I–85 you will see the entrance to Route 11, also called **Cherokee Foothills Scenic Highway.** If you can spare the time, this beautiful 130-mile road through the heart of the state's Blue Ridge Mountains will take you back to I–85 on the other side of the state. The following are a few of the incredible vistas along the way.

Caesar's Head has been a resort since antebellum times. It features a rock that juts out from the mountainside more than 1,200 feet above the Saluda River valley. Literature and exhibits are available at the visitor center here that describe the natural history of the area, with particular emphasis on the trails systems and the history of the early settlers. Call (864) 836–6115.

Raven Cliff Falls, located off Route 276 near Greenville County, is a 420-foot-high cascade in the Mountain Bridge Wilderness and Recreation Area and is one of the most breathtaking waterfalls in South Carolina. A 2-mile hike is necessary to reach the area.

Sassafras Mountain, which stands 3,560 feet high, is the highest point in South Carolina. From the top, four states can be viewed: Tennessee, North Carolina, South Carolina, and Georgia.

The *Chattooga National Wild and Scenic River,* another highlight of the Cherokee Foothills Scenic Highway, is a mecca for whitewater enthusiasts.

Nantahala Outdoor Center at 13077 Highway 19 West, Bryson City, NC, is licensed to take groups on the Chattanooga River for whitewater excitement. Call (703) 488–6900 for schedules. Wildwater, Ltd. proudly announces that they have safely carried more than 300,000 guests on their half-day, full-day, and two-day trips on the Chattooga. Trips on Section 3 of the Chattooga are perfect for families and youth groups. Section 4 is for the more advanced and more adventuresome. Call (864) 647–9587.

From Gaffney due east on Routes 29 and 5 the next stop is York, which was settled by the Scots and the Irish in the 1700s. For a time in the 1920s and 1930s, the Barnett Brothers' Circus made its winter quarters here. Back then every Christmas the shopping season was officially opened with a parade in which Santa Claus, escorted by the high school band, came swaying down Congress Street perched high above the crowd on the back of an elephant. Even today, it's said a few of the milky-white dogs of the town are descended from the long line of somersaulting terriers of the old circus.

In any event, York is a unique and charming town. *The McCelvey Center,* 212 East Jefferson Street, is a 580-seat performing arts theater and the center-piece of the community's cultural activities. *Summerfest,* a daylong extrava-ganza of children's activities, craft fairs, a classic car show, and a fireworks display, is held here on the fourth Saturday in August. It has been designated as one of the top twenty events in the entire Southeast. During the second weekend in December, the town hosts *Christmas in Olde York,* when the historic houses, of which there are many, are open to visitors, and the quaint streets are lit by luminarias for candlelight tours. There's more on York's activi-ties at www.yorkdowntown.com.

York is full of surprises, and one is the *Museum of York County,* a few miles east off Route 161 at 4621 Mount Gallant Road, Rock Hill. Watch for the museum signs—they'll lead you right there. The museum features the world's largest collection of mounted African hoofed animals, which are displayed in huge dioramas. My favorite is the rampaging elephant, which is rearing up at least 20 feet and swinging its tusks to the sky. Small kids go wild with this one. The museum also has a planetarium and a nature trail. Admission is $2.00 for adults, $1.00 for children. Open Monday through Saturday from 9:00 a.m. to 5:00 p.m. and Sunday from 1:00 to 5:00 p.m.; closed for major holidays. Call (803) 329–2121.

A few miles south of York on Route 1, visit **Brattonville.** This is a restored village of eighteenth- and nineteenth-century structures erected by several generations of the Bratton family. The homes are furnished with many Bratton pieces, including such items as an old-time biscuit press and a tin bath. One of the structures is a replica of a 1750 dirt-floored backwoodsman's cabin, complete with furniture and kitchen utensils. This restoration is open only on Tuesday, Thursday, and Sunday. Call (803) 684–2327 before you go because the schedule is subject to change. On the other hand, if you get there and everything is closed, you can always walk around the grounds and peer in through the windows. Admission is $4.00 for adults from out of the country (strange), $2.00 for adults who live in the country, and $1.00 for students age eighteen and under.

Nearby Rock Hill is a relatively large town with a population of 40,000. Also settled by Scots and Irish, Rock Hill's name came from the hard rock the railroaders had to deal with when they were laying tracks. Perhaps the most prestigious attraction here is the beautifully designed and wonderfully situated **Winthrop University.** The lush campus, spread out under magnificent oaks and magnolias, is so pleasant you'll want to stroll into every corner of it. Be sure to do so—everybody does. While you stroll, note the **Little Chapel,** the building where the school started. Designed and built by America's first architect, Robert Mills, the Little Chapel originally was in Columbia. In 1936 it was moved here brick by brick. Mills later went on to Washington to design and help build the Washington Monument. There's more on Winthrop at www.winthrop.edu.

Rock Hill has a new formal entrance called **The Gateway,** which looks as if it should be guarding Lenin's tomb on Red Square or in storage at Universal Studios for use in an epic Roman movie. Two 60-foot Egyptian pillars and four 13-foot bronze statues have been artistically arranged around a circular plaza on David Lyles Boulevard—the effect is one of painful solemnity. New York sculptor Audrey Flack has created the four identical statues of muscular maidens, each holding aloft a symbol of Rock Hill's many accomplishments. According to the inscriptions on the statues' stone bases, the fire is symbolic of the flame of knowledge; the circle of stars represents the city's attention to culture; the set of gears symbolizes Rock Hill's business growth; and the bolt of lightning points out the role the production of electricity has had in Rock Hill's development. I parked here and read every word on every monument and came away convinced that this was the work of a very, very large committee. The kids will love it, but don't make them write a paper on it. There's much more on Rock Hill at www.ci.rock-hill.sc.

Paramount's **Carowinds** is a hundred-acre water and theme park that straddles the North Carolina–South Carolina state line. Located on Carowinds Boulevard, Fort Mill, the park offers more than forty state-of-the-art rides, shows, and movie-themed experiences for all ages. Just take Interstate 77 to exit 90 at the North Carolina–South Carolina border. The park is just fifteen minutes south of uptown Charlotte, North Carolina, and 12 miles north of Rock Hill, South Carolina. More than thirty restaurants and snack stands provide a broad variety of dining choices, and the place is absolutely perfect for kids. They even have a gigantic wave pool. Call (803) 548–5300. Carowinds' Web site is www2.paramountparks.com/carowinds/. Or you can write to P.O. Box 410289, Charlotte, NC 28241.

The Columbia Plateau

As you approach Columbia on I–77, the red clay rises slightly and begins to flatten out. Wildflowers, crepe myrtle, and even azaleas are planted in the median. And then you see it—the brand-new skyline with the copper dome of the old capitol building in the center. The city is on a wide, flat plateau that was once a plantation owned by one Mr. J. T. Taylor, who went public with the outcry: "They ruined a damn fine plantation and built a sorry-assed town." Probably the most scenic drive into the old city, over the great rivers that meet here, is from the west on Jarvis Klapman Boulevard—a name that doesn't exactly trip lightly over the tongue. Not too long ago we had a rash of avenues, bridges, landfills, and runoff culverts unfortunately named for politicians who were, and are, still in office. And recently a committee has actually named a wide, tree-lined, beautiful avenue Colonial Life Boulevard.

But there it is—Columbia. Its gold and silver buildings and its copper dome stand under the reflecting clouds, illuminated like something out of a fairy tale or Disney World or the Land of Oz. The city is a study in contrasts. Out on the fringe you can still find combination general stores and service stations that sell night crawlers, bloodworms, and crickets to the anglers and candy from a curved glass case to the kids. You'll see smoked hams and mule collars along with fan belts and plow points hanging from the ceilings. Out front between the gas pumps will be the slick wooden bench where the old-timers still play checkers with bottle caps and watch the traffic going by.

Against these rustic reminders of the 1930s, the 1940s, and the 1950s, the city claims fifteen-story buildings of steel and colored glass, gourmet restaurants, three ballet companies, and a very fine South Carolina Shakespeare Company that performs for free in the city parks. The airport even offers nonstop air service to New York City and one-stop service to Los Angeles. And, just eight blocks west of the State House—in the center of the city— the Congaree River runs by the State Museum and Congaree Vista Park. It's right here in the Congaree that you can, with just a few arrangements, take a crack at catching a striped bass. The record was set fairly recently—forty-eight pounds. This is something you won't find in too many cities out there in the great Republic.

Columbia is the home of the **University of South Carolina,** which has grown from an enrollment of 4,000 students in the 1950s to a present-day student body of more than 39,400 at the campus in the heart of town. USC has a medical school and a law school, and for the past few years, the USC School of International Business has been rated among the nation's best by *U.S. News and World Report.* See a good profile of USC at www.sc.edu/aboutusc.

The city prides itself on the state-of-the-art **Richland County's Main Library,** an architectural masterpiece on four levels, each approximately one acre. This more than 39,400-square-foot building is one of the largest for an urban community of its size in the Southeast. The beautiful steel and glass construction with wonderful natural lighting and a forest of trees is truly all a library should be. The centerpiece here is the permanent art on the Garden Library, a 40-foot mural 18 feet high depicting the "wild rumpus scene" and two freestanding characters, all from Maurice Sendak's children's classic *Where the Wild Things Are.* This is the first time Sendak has authorized such use of his work as public art. The work is not only a wonderful background for the children's area but has been so designed and painted to allow the children to touch it. If you're traveling with kids, put the library on the top of your list. Call (803) 799–9084 or visit www.richland.lib.sc/main.cfm.

The city also has eight theaters, an enormous and beautiful inner-city park, the very successful Philharmonic Society, and the very fine **Columbia Museum of Art.** Located in the center of town at 1600 Main Street, the museum offers one of the better permanent collections of Baroque and Impressionist art in the entire Southeast. Among the artists represented are Monet, Matisse, Renoir, and such regional artists as Elizabeth O'Neill Verner from Charleston and Jasper Johns, who is from the Columbia area. The museum is open Tuesday through Saturday from 10:00 a.m. to 5:00 p.m. and Sunday from 1:00 to 5:00 p.m. On Wednesday the museum is open from 10:00 a.m. to 9:00 p.m. Closed on Monday. Admission is $5.00 for adults, $2.00 for students and senior citizens, and children age five and under get in free. Call (803) 799–2810. There's more at www.colmusart.org.

A recent addition to the USC campus and the city is the Koger Center, a remarkable 4,000-seat auditorium with one of the best stages in the country. It's located at 1051 Greene Street. See what's happening there at www.koger.sc .edu, or call (803) 777–7500. Even more recent is the completion of a beltway around the entire city that connects three interstates and joins Columbia—via I–77, I–26, and I–20—to Charleston, Greenville, and Charlotte, North Carolina.

Only eleven other cities in the nation share this style of highway transportation system. Now you can drive nonstop from Cleveland all the way to Charleston.

Thirty years ago the only ethnic food you could get in the old Columbia was pizza or maybe a Greek salad. Now, owing to the university's growing number of Asian students and the cosmopolitan population of the army stationed nearby at Fort Jackson, every cuisine from Vietnamese to Turkish to Indian to take-out sushi is available here. The schools have been integrated since the 1960s and are working as smoothly as those anywhere in the United States—they may, in fact, be better than most. And, at a time when whites-only country clubs are still flourishing across the nation, five of Columbia's six clubs are integrated.

The first stop should be the *South Carolina State Museum* at 301 Gervais Street. The building is an old cotton mill, and the floors are foot-thick maple, which was needed to support the heavy textile machinery. This state-of-the-art museum has marvelous exhibits about natural history, science, and technology, with hands-on displays for kids. They can light up a laser beam, talk into the whisper dish and hear their voices across the room, and even handle the fossilized teeth of an extinct mastodon. The transportation display has an ancient 1904 Oldsmobile as well as a modern space suit worn by General Charles M. Duke Jr., an astronaut from South Carolina. Open Tuesday through Saturday 10:00 a.m. to 5:00 p.m. and Sunday from 1:00 to 5:00 p.m. Adults pay $5.00, children age three to twelve, $3.00; free for children age two and under. Call (803) 898–4921. The Web site is www.museum.state.sc.us.

On up Gervais another block is *Longhorn Steakhouse,* at 902A Gervais Street, which advertises: NO QUICHE, NO FERNS. Instead they have country music, enough neon for a state fair, and the best steaks in town, with a very good salad for a modest price. This is a big place with many tables and booths. The service is excellent, and the prices are under $15. Call (803) 254–5100. For the other area Longhorn locations, see www.longhornsteakhouse.com.

One of the best but only slightly off-the-beaten path restaurants in the Vista Alley area is *The Motor Supply Company* at 920 Gervais Street. Ten years ago the building that now houses the restaurant was an auto-parts warehouse and store. When the management of the restaurant bought and began renovating the building, they found the old motor supply sign in the basement. It proved so irresistible that not only was the name used but the sign itself now hangs over the main door. Of special interest on the inside is an enormous oak back bar with marble columns that look as if they came out of a Roman bath.

This upscale restaurant features chicken, lamb, veal, steak, and a variety of pasta dishes and is locally famous for its desserts. They also have a wide range of very good wines. Prices are around $15 for lunch and range from $20 to $25 for dinner. Open for lunch Tuesday through Saturday 11:30 a.m. to 2:30 p.m.; dinner is served from 6:00 to 10:00 p.m. Tuesday through Thursday, 6:00 to 11:00 p.m. Friday and Saturday, and 6:00 to 10:00 p.m. Sunday. Closed Monday. Sunday brunch is served from 11:00 a.m. to 3:00 p.m. Sunday night is Thai night, from 5:00 to 11:00 p.m. Call (803) 256–6687 for reservations or just drop in. Their Web site is www.motorsupplycobistro.com.

A block west of Motor Supply at 804 Gervais is *Adluh Milling Company,* which produces flour, meals, corn-bread mix, and another dozen milled products. Their old red neon has been burning high on the roof over Columbia for as long as most people can remember. Adluh is owned by the Allen brothers, who have made a career out of supporting education in the state through donations and scholarships to colleges and universities. The factory itself offers guided tours for schoolchildren, Scouts, senior citizens, and other groups. Each tour is capped with a visit to their hospitality room, where biscuits or hush puppies are baked right before your eyes, from the flour you just saw made, and served with butter, jams, and jellies. If you'd like to get on one of these tours, which will take you through the mill and show you how flour and the various milled products are made, one of the staff will try to join you up with a group. By the way, "Adluh" is "Hulda" backwards. Call (803) 779–2460. Visit www.adluh.com/history.htm.

A few blocks from Adluh Flour is *Miyo's* at 922 South Main. This is a very fine restaurant specializing in Shanghai and Szechuan cuisine, located right in the center of the city. Michelle and Yong Wang, both from New York City, moved here a few years ago and have quickly moved into the absolute top spot in the entire county for Chinese cooking. They have a beautiful mahogany bar where they serve hot and chilled sake, liquor, and fine wines. They have recently remodeled and refurnished the old building so that now, along with the delicious food, you can sit in a stunning setting of Oriental art. Hours are Monday through Saturday, lunch 11:30 a.m. to 2:30 p.m. except on Saturday, dinner 5:30 to 10:00 p.m. Prices are $8.00 for lunch, $10.00 to $20.00 for dinner. You can also call ahead for take-out service. Call (803) 779–6496 or visit www.miyos.com.

You can't miss the *State House* on the corner of Main and Gervais; it's in the center of everything. This blue granite building was shelled by Sherman in 1865 from across the Congaree River. The spots where the shells landed are marked on the western side of the building with bronze stars. On the steps of the capitol is a bronze statue of George Washington, with his cane broken off. The story and the inscription tell us the Union forces "brickbatted it." You can go inside and take the free tour conducted from 9:00 a.m. to noon and from

A Very Short History of South Carolina Football

Right smack in the middle of the dog days of September, when the northern trans-plants are wondering when, and if, the summer will ever end, the madness begins. We break out our Gamecock jackets, caps, and banners, and start politicking for a parking space within 1,000 yards of Williams-Brice Stadium. And then it's Saturday and there we are, where we've been sitting forever, watching Gamecock football. The game goes on and the stouthearted fans, of ten, twenty, thirty—you name it—years cheer and shout, groan, and scream all the way into the fourth quarter. And then as if on signal, when we're fourteen or twenty-one or twenty-seven or thirty-six points behind, they begin silently filing out and looking forward to the next game and the game after that, as they have been doing since the days when Pitchfork Ben Tillman was ravaging the countryside.

Looking down the ninety-year-old Spanish moss–draped tunnel of Gamecock foot-ball, there is one grim and comic statistic that is seldom reported by the local press. Our best year (except 1984) was 1903—seven wins and three losses. But one of the victories was against the Columbia-based YMCA and the other, an 89 to 0 humiliation of the Welsh Neck High School.

But all this changed in 1984, when we won five in a row and were rated up there with the name brands in the Associated Press Poll. I covered the games that year and here are the notes from my journal: "Back in the not-so-long-ago days of '83, '82, '81, and '80, right about now we'd be three wins and three losses, and we'd be looking forward to basketball and the winter solstice. But this year was different. This was too crazy to believe. We actually had a football team. We'd always had a football team, but this one was winning. We were actually undefeated in five straight games and were right up there on page one of the sports section in the New York Times, the L.A. Times, and the Chicago Tribune. Right up there with Nebraska, Oklahoma, Texas, Ohio State: schools with ball teams that get on national television and go to bowl games. Schools where the old grads die and leave oil wells and skyscrapers and coastlines to the Athletic Department. Serious big time, household names like Michigan, Penn State, Southern Cal, and Notre Dame."

But now we were winning. The fever had hit Columbia, and we were twisting and trembling in torment. New and terrible, weird things were happening all over

1:30 to 3:30 p.m. Open Monday through Friday 9:00 a.m. to 4:00 p.m. Call (803) 734–2430, or visit www.scstatehouse.net.

A block south at 1012 Sumter Street, just behind the State House, is *Town Theatre.* While the building is only one hundred years old, the theater has the distinguished record of running continuously for more than eighty-five years. The actors, directors, and stagehands are all local citizens. Call (803) 799–2510 for current schedules or check out www.towntheatre.com.

town—we were out of control. Housebreaking and embezzling and brutal crimes dipped twenty to twenty-five points, but freak accidents increased by thirty. Cars were piling into hedges, phone poles, and runoff culverts; others simply left the road as if "The Rapture" was upon them, and they could be seen out in the fresh rows of collards and soybeans. But it wasn't "The Rapture" or the fear of a first strike by the Red Menace, poised somewhere down there in the jungles of Guadalajara. It was pure, cold-biscuit-down-in-the-dirt Gamecock Fear. Our next game was with Notre Dame at Notre Dame, and if by some miracle we won, we would have six wins in a row and be among the top three in the country. At the bars, prayer groups, and Tupperware parties, you could feel the fear. You could hear it.

"Hell, I'm breaking out in a Gamecock Rash."

"I need four drinks to feel one."

"My teeth feel soft and the back of my hands itch."

And one howling looper at the end of the bar banged on it two times, three times, four. "I've had it. You hear me? I can't go on like this! I'm calling Jim Holderman and I'm telling him to stop the damn season and send me the bill."

Anyhow, we beat Notre Dame, then N.C. State, then Florida State, and were eight in a row with no losses and right up there at number two in the A.P. Poll. We lost the next game to Navy, but then we beat Clemson and went down to the Gator Bowl, where we lost in the last minute to Oklahoma State. The season ended with nine wins and two losses—the best season ever—and now, more than sixteen years later, we still haven't recovered. And may never recover. Even today you can see faded garnet and black bumper stickers pleading and screaming, "Wait till '84!"

And why am I telling you all this? I'll tell you why. For the past thirty or forty years, it has been impossible to get Gamecock tickets. But now that has changed, for in 1998 we started a losing streak of twenty-one games, which has probably broken every college record on the books. And for the first time in a long, long time, tickets are available. So call the Athletic Department at (803) 777–4274 for the schedule and tickets, and come on out to Williams-Brice. You'll never, ever forget it. If you can't get through, try www.ticketcity.com.southcarolinagamecockstickets.

The *Trustus Theater* at 520 Lady Street is another interesting theater, providing deep comfortable couches as well as soft drinks, beer, and popcorn for the audiences. First-class entertainment and professionally acted and staged plays are always on the playbill here. Call (803) 254–9732 for their current schedule. Their Web site is www.trustus.org.

Two blocks north of the capitol is the *Equitable Arcade Building* at 1332 Main Street. This amazing and beautiful structure, built in Second Renaissance

notsofast!

One night back in the 1960s, Satchel Paige, the famous baseball pitcher, was stopped by the police in the middle of Gervais Street for speeding. When the police recognized him, and after he gave them a stack of autographed eight-by-elevens for their friends and families, they formed a motorcade around his big Cadillac and escorted him on across and out onto the highway to Atlanta.

Revival style in 1912, was Columbia's first enclosed shopping mall. It is now on the National Register of Historic Places. Shaped like an "L" with ornamental facades both on Main Street and around the corner on Washington Street, the two-story Arcade has a central hallway lighted by an enormous skylight. The facing is white terra-cotta marble and decorated ceramic tile. Six huge double-tiered bronze chandeliers provide evening lighting. With all the glass and light and white marble, the old building looks not unlike the galleries of Florence or Venice. It's a downtown tragedy that the building, probably the most delicate, attractive, and unique structure in the entire city, hasn't been renovated and put to better use. In any event, stop by and walk through. You'll never see anything quite like it again.

Gracie's Tea Room is the brightest bright spot in the old Arcade. Gracie serves wonderful sandwiches, salads, and baked goods. Everything is around $3.00 to $4.00, and you can also take home whole cakes and pies or some of her famous homemade bread. They do a brisk business here and for a very good reason—everything is not only modestly priced but very, very good. Open for lunch only Monday through Friday from 11:30 a.m. to 2:30 p.m. Closed Saturday and Sunday. You can give Gracie's a call at (803) 254–7913.

On the corner of Richland and Pickens is *Seibel's House,* the oldest house in Columbia. Built in 1796, it is surrounded by palmetto trees. A separate kitchen built of handmade bricks stands behind the house, and there's a large and

Seibel's House

beautiful garden at the side. Today the house is the administrative headquarters of the Historic Columbia Foundation. They're located at 1601 Richland Street. Their helpful Web site is www.historiccolumbia.org. Call (803) 252–7742.

Within walking distance from Seibel's House is the ticket office for all the house museums under the auspices of Historic Columbia Foundation. It's in one of the outbuildings associated with the **Robert Mills House and Park** at 1616 Blanding Street. Robert Mills is the architect who designed the Washington Monument in our nation's capital, among other important landmarks in Columbia and around South Carolina. Tickets are $5.00 per house for adults; $4.00 for college students, seniors 65 or older, and active duty military personnel. For ages six through seventeen, the cost is $3.00; and under age six it's free. Hours are 9:00 a.m. to 5:00 p.m. Monday through Friday. The Web site is www.historiccolumbia.org/historic/mills.html.

Next door at 1615 Blanding is the **Hampton-Preston Mansion,** home of the Wade Hampton family. The first Wade Hampton served in the Revolutionary War and was a general in the War of 1812; Wade Hampton II was an officer in the War of 1812; and Wade Hampton III commanded the Confederate cavalry during the Civil War and later became governor of South Carolina.

Mann-Simon Cottage, at 1403 Blanding, was the home of Celia Mann, a slave from Charleston who purchased her freedom with money she earned as a midwife. She walked to Columbia, bought this wooden cottage, and made her home here until her death years later. Today the ground floor is a gallery of artwork where local African-American artists display their art for viewing and purchasing. Books and gifts are available in the gallery.

"most famous dropout"

My old high school, Columbia High, awarded the "Most Famous Graduate" honor to Cardinal Joseph Bernadin. But coming up hard on the outside track was yours truly with "Most Famous Dropout." Since the Cardinal was too busy with Scriptures to speak at the dedication of the school's new building a few years back, I was chosen. There's a moral here someplace, but I can't put my finger on it.

Woodrow Wilson's Boyhood Home, at 1705 Hampton Street, is another museum house presented by Historic Columbia Foundation. However, an extensive restoration program is currently under way there, which will keep this site closed until sometime in 2009. Still, this is a fascinating place to see—if only from the outside. When done, the house will display many Wilson family pieces, including the bed in which Woodrow Wilson was born. Wilson's father, Joseph Ruggles Wilson, was a Presbyterian minister; he and his wife are buried only a few blocks away at Columbia's First Presbyterian Church, where Reverend Wilson served.

Another two dozen historic sites in Columbia are worth seeing. Among the most notable are **Tapp's Department Store, Lexington State Bank, Sylvan's Jewelry,** the **Governor's Mansion** on Richland Street, and the **Lace House** directly across from it.

Modeled on the open-pit design of the San Diego Zoo, **Riverbanks Zoological Park** is rated one of the top ten zoos in the country year after year. Its budget is more than $4 million a year, and it houses more than 2,000 animals in natural settings without cages. In addition, more than 1,000 reptiles, amphibians, and fish from around the world are housed in an aquarian-reptile complex. Located at 500 Wildlife Parkway, the Saluda River runs between the zoo and the Botanical Gardens, and the anglers who hear the animal calls at night or in the early morning say it's like being on the Amazon. Kids love the huge seal and sea lion pool, especially at feeding time. Very good outdoor snack bars serve almost anything you like for lunch. If you're one of those people who is going to drive from Cleveland to Charleston on the interstates and you can only make one stop in Columbia, I'd make it the zoo. You can't go wrong: Recently the zoo has expanded its facilities and is now housing four gorillas, three koala bears, and an elaborate bird exhibit where you purchase nectar for $1.00 and South American birds will drink it right out of your hand. Kids love it. Be sure to bring your camera along because the shots of the kids feeding the birds are wonderful. Very safe for all ages. Open daily 9:00 a.m. to 4:00 p.m. Admission is $9.75 for adults (age thirteen and over); $7.25 for children three to twelve; children age two and under admitted free. For further information call (803) 779–8717. For more on Riverbanks Zoo, visit www.riverbanks.org.

Back on Main Street, 6 blocks north of the capitol (1734 Main Street) stop at **Aqua Grill,** which is more than just a grill where they serve fish. This is a very upscale restaurant with an elaborate wine list and a wonderful menu. While seafood is the main fare here, there is also steak and chicken, and everything is served in a truly different dining atmosphere. The ceiling has been designed and sculpted to resemble the surface of the ocean, and directly above you is a series of metal sculptures of fish ranging from 4 feet long to one enormous one of at least 25 feet. The entire place makes you think you are looking up from the ocean floor. It really has to be seen to be appreciated. They offer at least fifteen varieties of wine that can be ordered by the glass. The bar picks up the undersea motif with a series of fish tanks built into the supporting columns with beautiful yellow and blue tropical fish. There is also outdoor seating for the bar, overlooking the palm trees and young oaks that line Main Street. Altogether, this is a marvelous place to dine. Dinner prices range from $16 to $21. There's

A Few More Words about Barbecue

For some reason rednecks down here in the "hard lard belt" are now billing their barbecue as "gourmet barbecue." But it's a free country and you can call it anything you want. Anyhow, there are a few not-so-well-known facts I thought I'd pass along to the tourists and the transplants to raise their sensitivity and make them much better consumers. Basically there are three classifications for barbecue hogs: the three rib down, the five rib down, and the seven rib down. This is the butcher's term that tells you how much a rack of ribs weighs. What this also tells you is the three rib down comes from a smaller hog that has less fat than the five rib, and considerably less than the seven rib down hog. The result of all this is that the three rib down is smaller and thinner and has less fat and is obviously tastier. As a result, three rib down is much more expensive, harder to find, and is really the only truly "gourmet barbecue." A basic rule would be that a buffet of "All You Can Eat Barbecue" that has to withstand the seismic charge of entire football teams will probably be five rib down. Meanwhile, out at the fair and political fund-raising functions where the beer drinkers will eat anything, there is a strong chance it'll be the fatter seven rib down.

I guess it all boils down to this. The next time someone tells you about "gourmet barbecue," ask what kind of hogs he or she uses. They will say, what do you mean? And you answer "Well, judging by the length and weight of this here rib and all this fat dripping on my leisure suit . . ."

more on this "undersea" dining adventure at www.aquagrilleandlounge.com. Open 11:30 a.m. to 2:00 p.m. for lunch, 5:30 to 11:00 p.m. for dinner Tuesday through Saturday. Closed Sunday and Monday. Call (803) 376–8888.

Home of the finest mustard-based, sauce-drenched barbecue in the Southeast, **Piggie Park** is so famous that its product is shipped to every state in the country and all over the world. Almost as famous is Maurice Bessinger, the owner and operator. During the 1950s he was an ardent segregationist; in the 1960s he found Jesus and became a leading integrationist. Next he ran for governor on a white horse and lost, and then, discovering something in Scripture, he turned his Barbecue Buffeteria into a mission for the gospel.

Maurice can't seem to stay out of trouble and the public eye. His recent flap has been that he will not remove his Confederate flag from the top of his restaurant. But recent negotiations have resulted in his lowering it under the Stars and Stripes and the State Palmetto Flag. Despite this, stop in here anyway. The food is excellent; you don't have to load up on religious tracts or listen to Maurice. And if you're lucky he'll stop by your table and tell you a lot more than you're willing to listen to about the old Confederacy. Maurice practices what he preaches: good food at a reasonable price and an unswerving belief in every word of the Scriptures. Eat one of his "Little Joe" barbecue sandwiches with a side of the best onion rings you'll ever eat. Back when Al McGuire coached Marquette and they came to town to play USC's Gamecocks, his first stop in town was Maurice's. Joseph Heller, author of *Catch 22,* loved it, and so does Nora Ephron, who directed *Sleepless in Seattle,* and so did the late Mickey Spillane, who lived down the road in Murrells Inlet. During Desert Storm the 240th Combat Communications Squadron from nearby McEntire Air Base asked Maurice to send some barbecue to Kuwait. Maurice couldn't fill that order, but when the 200 men returned to Columbia he gave them and their spouses a free all-they-could-eat barbecue meal at the base. Open Monday through Thursday 10:00 a.m. to 11:00 p.m. and Friday and Saturday 10:00 a.m. to midnight. The main store is at 1600 Charleston Highway. Call (803) 796–0220 or visit www .mauricesbbq.com for the location nearest you.

Five Points, a mile or so southeast of the capitol, is the city's main center of activity. Here the university students gather to pound their drums and string their beads. At 2007 Devine, right in the heart of Five Points, is **Portfolio Art Gallery.** This is a small but packed-to-the-ceiling store that carries a huge variety of paintings, sculptures, blown-glass pieces, jewelry, and clay, wood, and paper pieces. Judith Roberts, who taught art in the local public school and is the owner, won national notice a few years back when she worked with a group of handicapped students, whose ages ranged from preschool to twenty-one years, on a huge 10-by-12-foot mural of animals and shrubs. Not only did it win the state competition, but it was eventually displayed at the Kennedy Center in Washington, D.C.

Judith says, "I'm really not a terrific salesperson but I get excited talking about art, and I feel that most people like to talk about the paintings that interest them. They like to know something about the artist and why they respond favorably to his or her work. That's what I talk to them about—why a piece appeals to them, and I use basic compositional values in explaining its interest. Sometimes at midnight, I'll have twelve people in here. I've sold a painting at 1:00 in the morning." Hours are 10:00 a.m. to 6:00 p.m. Monday through Saturday. Check out her Web site at www.portfolioartgal.com.

The **Blue Cactus Cafe** in Five Points is definitely a must. Located at 2002H Greene Street, the restaurant's decor is eclectic, with a sombrero hanging from the ceiling, a bookcase of hot sauces, postcards from customers from around the world, a world map with pins to show where customers are from, and a little display of snuff cans (very funky)—and this is just the beginning. Recommended lunch fare would be the *be bim bop* (basically a bowl of rice with an assortment of Korean-style vegetables on top); a choice of beef, chicken, or tofu; and usually an egg served on top of that—you break the egg on top and mix it all up. (Request what you want or don't want on it!) For dinner, try the curry chicken stir fry (the owner's own recipe). Dinner for two, with appetizers and drinks, will cost under $20. And don't forget the tasty appetizers: *kim bob* (Korean seaweed roll—all vegetable) or Korean dumplings (meat, cabbage, clear noodles). You can always top off your meal with a bowl of Japanese adzuki ice cream, green tea, or ginger ice cream. The Blue Cactus is truly a family-run place: Lloyd and Mary Reese are the owners and chefs; Mary's sisters and sisters-in-law help out in the back; and a slew of cousins and children help run the place as well. Go early, because they tend to get packed (the food is excellent!), and, as Lloyd's daughter laughingly says, "We're horribly slow, but Dad would say 'arrogantly' slow!" On a scale of five stars or spoons or forks, or whatever, the Blue Cactus would surely get ten of everything! Call (803) 929–0782 or visit www.bluecactuscafe.com.

You'll find ***Claussen's Inn*** at 2003 Greene Street a unique, comfortable, and very attractive place to stay. The old brick building used to be a bakery, and you can still see the logo in the bricks at the front. Inside, the twenty-nine rooms have 20-foot ceilings, and the loft suites have winding staircases. In 1995, when William Styron, Joe Heller, William Manchester, Paul Fussel, James Dickey, Mickey Spillane, and Al Wertheim were in Columbia for a conference, they all stayed here. Rates are from $120 to $150 with a continental breakfast and refreshments in the afternoon. Claussen's is 4 blocks from the university and 100 yards from the center of Five Points. Call (803) 765–0440. Their Web address is www.claussensinn.com.

Down the hill about 100 yards from Claussen's is ***Garibaldi's,*** 2013 Greene Street. This is a first-class restaurant with an excellent wine list, a menu that changes daily, superb food, and a very fine staff. My favorite dish is the apricot-smothered, baked-to-a-crisp flounder. The bar is comfortable for long waits, and you have a fine view of Five Points. Prices for dinner range from $12 to $30. Open for dinner Sunday through Thursday from 5:30 to 10:30 p.m. and on Friday and Saturday from 5:30 to 11:00 p.m. Call (803) 771–8888.

Across the street and a little farther down the hill is ***Yesterday's Restaurant and Tavern,*** 2030 Devine Street. Out front up on the roof is a cowboy sitting in a bathtub with his ten-gallon hat and his boots and spurs on, which is an indicator of the inside atmosphere. Two televisions serve the bar and the local sports fans and university students. The rest of the space has booths and tables, and during lunch they're packed. Here's an idea for you. Skip a couple meals and come here and order the Confederate fried steak. It's served with white gravy, any three vegetables you can name, and all the corn bread you can handle. It will not only stick to every rib you've ever had, but it's as close to delicious as anything you'll ever eat. Open Sunday through Tuesday from 11:30 to 1:00 a.m.; Wednesday through Saturday from 11:30 to 2:00 a.m. Call (803) 779–0196, or visit www.yesterdayssc.com.

Yesterday's Restaurant and Tavern

Leaving Yesterday's by the side door, you are directly in front of **Goat-feathers** at 2017 Devine Street, an excellent coffeehouse that serves a lot more than just coffee. You can get a whole meal here of soup and French bread, fresh bagels, or fresh croissants. You can get almost any dessert ever created. Goatfeathers is unquestionably one of the best and liveliest bars in town. A round table in the middle of the room seats ten and is loaded with magazines and newspapers. While you're waiting for a table, you can flip through the reading material or go next door to the unique **Intermezzo Book Store,** which is owned by Goatfeathers. Browse through their selection of newspapers and magazines from France, Italy, Germany, Israel, and other countries— more than twenty international papers. Recently they've installed a cigar bar with at least forty varieties from all over the world. They also have a good supply of Batman Zippo lighters. They're at (803) 799–2276.

Someone once said that the South knows as much about cooking veal as a hog knows about the Lord's plan for salvation. I shall now lay that myth to rest. At **Dianne's,** 2400 Devine Street, just up the hill from Five Points, they make a veal piccata that rivals anything in the five boroughs of New York. The very thin milk-fed veal is sautéed in a light egg batter with fresh herbs and finished with white wine, lemon, and capers. It is a joy and a wonder. The other veals crossing the finish line with colors flying here are: parmigiana, marsala, saltimbocca, Antoinette, and Fellini. The Caesar salad here is first rate, as is every one of the appetizers. A good suggestion is to have two appetizers, a salad, and a good bottle of wine. They also have air-conditioned patio dining. Closed Monday. And don't forget to tell Dianne I sent you.

On Wednesday night the popular Ross Holmes and his band play Beach Music, show tunes, and standards and will play anything you can name. He does a great job of singing "Summer Wind" and almost anything Sinatra ever recorded. The prices here range from $6.00 for a small pizza to $40.00 for dinner. Great bar here, with interesting bartenders and a good supply of local characters. Try it, you can't go wrong. Hours for dining are Sunday through Thursday 5:00 to 10:00 p.m., Friday and Saturday 5:00 to 11:00 p.m. Her phone is (803) 254–3535; her Web site is http://dianesondevine.com.

The new surprise in Columbia for breakfast and lunch is ***Just Fresh Bakery Cafe*** at Suite 275 in the Capitol Center Building at 1201 Main Street. Every morning at 4:30 they begin baking their fine bread products, cleaning their produce for salads and sandwiches, preparing their soups, and grinding their highest quality coffee beans. Breakfast is served every morning. On their menu you will also find assorted muffins, banana nut bread, and croissants. Pay close attention to the assorted muffins. I had breakfast there for a solid fourteen running days determined to try everything. But on the first day I discovered their corn muffin—which comes with real corn kernels—and I looked no more. Fourteen days later I had had fourteen corn muffins with my fourteen Kona coffees. It's the perfect breakfast. I think I am now up around forty or fifty or sixty, still going strong, and absolutely convinced it's the best muffin in the Southeast Conference. If you like, you can walk it down the street to the fountain or sit out front under the big tree with the paper and watch the passing parade. Very pleasant. Very good. Don't miss it. Take-out service is first-class. Hours are Monday through Saturday 7:00 a.m. to 9:00 p.m., Sunday 8:00 a.m. to 3:00 p.m.; call (803) 771–4242 or visit www.justfresh.com.

McAllister's Deli has four places: one at 4710 Forest Drive (803–790–5995); one at 300 Columbiana Drive (803–781–4550); one at 119 Sparkleberry Lane (803–788–7600); and one more at 5175 Sunset Boulevard in Lexington (803–951–3332). All are excellent and have fine service and a wonderful menu of deli sandwiches, salads, soups, and desserts. Very good corned beef and pastrami sandwiches as well as excellent soups in a bread bowl, if you like. Very good lemonade. A money-saving "just for kids" menu is also available. Hours are 10:30 a.m. to 10:00 p.m. seven days a week.

Soaps. Here's something that's not only practical and reasonable but absolutely necessary. Here at 140 Assembly Street, near Capitol City Park, is a place where you can drop off your clothes for washing and folding and pick them up in a couple hours. If you like you can hang around and drink beer, watch TV, or lounge on the tanning beds. Kids are welcome, and two full-sized pool tables and all the video games they can handle are available. Ideal place to get the laundry done and read a magazine while you turn the kids loose for a while. Hours are 6:30 a.m. to 10:00 p.m. seven days a week. Call (803) 252–0005.

Groucho's at 611 Harden Street (803–779–5708) has the definite flavor of a New York deli. The pastrami and corned beef are excellent, and the service is fast and courteous. Great rye bread here along with any kind of beer and soft drink. This is a famous hangout for Carolina students that goes back a long, long time. Hours are 11:00 a.m. to 4:00 p.m. Monday through Saturday. Great take-out service. Check out their other locations in South Carolina at www.grouchosdeli.com.

Doug's Dogs, 124 Park Street (803–252–8143), is right in the center of the south end of Columbia but truly off the beaten path. Go west on Whaley, cross Assembly, and go one short block to Park Street. Turn left and there it is back under the trees. Outside there are a couple picnic tables and chairs where you can eat if you like. But go inside and talk to owners Doug and Nancy Hawkins. This is about as down home as it gets down here, and the prices will leave you standing there with your mouth open. Last time I was there, a BLT was $1.59, cheese sandwiches 99 cents, liver pudding sandwich 99 cents, and a very fine egg salad sandwich was 99 cents. The hot dogs are famous here and only 90 cents, or two for $1.70. Don't leave the place without at least trying a "hoe cake." This is a mixture of flour, eggs, water, and shortening that's fried in an iron pan. Some people swear by them. Not me. They're a trifle heavy, but that's the way they're designed. If you happen to lose one in the car and discover it a couple of weeks later, it will be as sturdy and as tasty as it was when it first crossed the counter. The name "hoe cake" springs from the fact that, when the farmers went out to hoe, they carried the cakes along in their pockets. Just try one bite. It's unforgettable, and you'll never tire of telling Yankees about it and showing them a sample. They keep forever. Doug's caters to a lot of construction workers from the town who love them, as well as the crews who work down the road at the **Vulcan Rock Quarry** a few blocks away. The hours are tricky: 5:30 a.m. to 2:30 p.m. Monday through Friday. Closed Saturday and Sunday.

A full day of off the beaten path while still in Columbia would be breakfast or lunch at Doug's, then, after you dropped your laundry off for washing, drying, and folding at Soap's, go down Whaley Street again until you hit Williams Street. Turn left here and ease down to the end where you will be in the heart of the PD: The following can be in regular/roman type **Vulcan Rock Quarry.** This is a one-of-a-kind phenomenon that everyone should see. Basically it's an old rock quarry where they have been digging out granite for over a hundred years. The heavy-duty trucks at the bottom will look like toys. The quarry, from where the granite is removed, is about a half-mile wide and 500 feet deep and is made up of 50-foot shelves staggered down the face of the pit. The breeze from the Congaree River only a few hundred yards away comes over the ridge and into the pit to create a vortex. While you can't see it, the buzzards, who have made a happy home here, can. Since they aren't too energetic to begin with, they love to sail around and around on the rising currents. You might see eight or ten at a time sailing along in their typical loose buzzard formation. Red-tailed hawks and eagles can also be spotted, and in the evening owls and red and gray foxes. This is a fascinating spectacle and it's right in the center of town. There's more on Vulcan's quarry operations at www.vulcanmaterials.com.

The Oyster Bar at 1123 Park Street, in the heart of the Vista, is precisely that, an oyster bar. There are no ferns, no side dishes, no sauces, no beds of lettuce and pasta, not even a garnish. Condiments, soup, and crackers are the only edibles on the table. Your waiter shucks your oysters and brings you drinks, and that's the way it's supposed to be. Oysters are $10.00 for half of a bucket. If you prefer steamed shrimp or scallops, they are priced at $18 a pound. Very friendly place, and if you go there you'll be back. Call (803) 799–4484. Hours are 4:00 to 11:00 p.m. Monday through Saturday.

Hampton Street Vineyard is a lovely restaurant at 1201 Hampton Street in downtown Columbia, catering to those who love fine dining, fine wining, and a relaxing time. *Wine Spectator* magazine gave it the prestigious "Best Award of Excellence," and there's a reason why—with over 650 different types of wines in stock, they're able to offer thirty-five wines by the glass! Unprecedented in our neck of the woods. And the food is simply delicious. Lunch served Monday through Friday 11:30 a.m. to 2:00 p.m. Dinner served Monday through Saturday 6:00 p.m. to 10:00 p.m. Smoking permitted at the bar, which opens at 5:00 p.m. Monday through Saturday. Call (803) 252–0850. Their whole menu is online at www.hamptonstreetvineyard.com.

Found in just about every major neighborhood in Columbia (we highly recommend the one on Beltline), *Lizard's Thicket* has turned into a Columbia institution. Those who are fans are either eating there now, are on the way to eat there, or have just finished eating there and are planning their next trip. Banana Pudding is the ultimate dessert, and if you don't want to cook on a major holiday, they open their doors with holiday fare. This is fast, inexpensive, home-cooked food (but not "fast-food"), with waitresses you'll want to adopt as aunts. The only downside of Lizard's Thicket is that they aren't in other parts of the United States—just another reason to come to South Carolina. (My sister-in-law makes annual trips down here from New York just so she can spend a week eating at Lizard's Thicket. She doesn't miss one meal—which makes it really easy on the wife.) Call (803) 738–0006 or check out their twelve locations at www.lizardsthicket.com.

Even though **Za's** is not considered a kid's restaurant, it's my kid's favorite Columbia hangout. She likes to take the dogs to lunch or dinner, stick their leashes on the patio chair, and order a pizza outside (the patio is a huge dining area in itself). She's been coming here since she was six months old, so she should know what's good—she orders the T-Zone, which is basically a sandwich pizza, served with either fresh fruit, chips, pasta salad, or coleslaw. Of course, everyone orders the fruit salad, because this is the sort of restaurant that serves really fresh fruit. Inside, the restaurant is attractive and big, without seeming to be too big—expect a good ambience, with low lighting, copper decor, and good-looking wait staff. Sunday lunch is a good time to go, because it isn't too crowded. Weekends you'll have to wait—proof of how really good this restaurant is—and it's worth the wait. It's at 2930 Devine Street (803–771–7334). Hours are Monday through Wednesday 11:30 a.m. to 10:00 p.m., Thursday and Friday 11:30 a.m. to 11:00 p.m., Saturday 11:30 a.m. to 10:00 p.m., and Sunday 11:30 a.m. to 9:00 p.m. Learn more at www.zasbrickovenpizza.com.

Don't expect to move much when you leave the table at **The Original Pancake House** at 4840 Forest Drive (803–782–6742). Pancakes come with everything, and they're so tasty you can't help eating them—all. The focus is on pancakes, but the crepes will make your teeth ache, they're so good. Be careful ordering the omelette, it's about the size of a football, and you'll be forced to eat the whole thing because it is a scientifically proven fact that a person can't stop until the last bite. In fact, everything is served fast (except on Sunday, when the church crowd hits), but expect to waddle out slowly—and satisfied. Visit www.originalpancakehouse.com.

I guess at some point I have to pick what I think is the best of the best restaurants in the old town. It's not quite off the beaten path; as a matter of fact, it's right smack in the middle of Five Points. It's called **Saluda's,** named for the river that runs through the town. The address is 751 Saluda Avenue (803–799–9500). First of all you have to climb twenty steps to get to it, but every single step is worth it because this has to be the best food and the best service in town. Second, it has the best view of Five Points, and the 20-foot fountain that is its centerpiece. Third, in the spring, summer, and fall, Saluda's helps sponsor a Wednesday evening music program, with big local and touring bands playing everything: jazz, rock, lite rock, bluegrass, and Broadway show tunes. Anyhow, when you're dining at Saluda's out on a beautiful terrace, you have the best seat in the house for the music, because you're literally looking down on it only 30 or 40 feet away.

Saluda's also has a private dining area that can host up to fifty people; ideal for bridal showers, business meetings, or any private party. Their main dining room can host up to 200 guests, depending on your seating arrangements.

Along with an extensive wine list of over 250 selections, the chef here offers an eclectic mix of American and continental cuisine. One of the specials is the huge lamb shank with a veal basil and demi-glaze. Another is a black and white sesame seed–crusted fillet of salmon, pan-seared and served over wasabi mashed potatoes, with a side of seasonal vegetables. The menu changes seasonally. You can check their Web site, www.saludas.com, to see what's new on the menu. Hours are Monday through Thursday 5:30 to 10:00 p.m., Friday and Saturday 5:30 to 10:30 p.m. Good tip: Show up here some evening for a cool cocktail out on the patio overlooking the fountain. And while you're here, find out what days the orchestra is playing and make your reservations.

One of the very best Devine Street dining delights is ***Birds On A Wire*** (2901 Devine Street; 803–254–2445). Here you will find the best chicken in town, served every way and then some. A coin toss will usually have to help you decide whether to take the Tabasco Chicken Pasta Salad or the pulled chicken with glorious sides, such as: sweet potatoes, mashed potatoes, collards, green beans, and more. If you don't want to eat inside you can enjoy your food on the big porch that is located to the side of the restaurant, next to a side street. (And even better, when you are finished, sneak around to the other side of the building to find Ben & Jerry's ice cream!) Hours are Monday through Saturday 11:30 a.m. to 10:00 p.m. Also open for Sunday brunch from 11:00 a.m. to 3:00 p.m.

The South's largest children's museum and the best in America is ***EdVenture*** at 211 Gervais Street. Walk into EdVenture, and the first thing you'll see is a giant 40-foot statue of a boy ("The World's Largest Child") sitting cross-legged, wearing a baseball cap, with kids crawling all over and inside him. His watch is an actual clock for the museum (although upside down!). His insides are a McDonald's Play Place–type sliding/climbing structure. But there's more. Go into his heart area and hear the beating pulse; the stomach rumbles and grumbles; and the brain's synapses snap, crackle, and pop, totally delighting those who have made it to the top. And this is just the beginning of the adventure at EdVenture. There's the farm room, complete with a milking cow, chickens that lay eggs, real tractors, and more. Cross over to the next room to climb into a real fire engine (put on some fire gear, too). Interested in being a sheriff or a builder? Want to change a real tire on a car? The tools are everywhere. Over to the other side of the building, as well as upstairs and outside, you'll find an Australian room (teaching you all sorts of Outback magic); a giant spider web in which to crawl around; a critter garden; a computer room; a dentist's office, where you can extract teeth; and the list just runs on and on. Admission is $8.95 for those thirteen and older, $6.95 for children from one through twelve; and it's free for babies under a year of age. Save money by purchasing a yearlong pass, because you will use it! The museum is open from 9:00 a.m. to 5:00 p.m., Tuesday through Saturday, and from noon to 5:00 p.m. on Sunday. For more information, go to www.edventure.org/museum.asp or call (803) 779–3100.

Lillian's at 4517 Forest Drive is the place in Columbia to have lunch if you're in the mood for a tea party. Not that they really focus on tea, because they do not, or that you have to dress up, because you don't—but the ambience of a grown-up tea party is there. Try the turkey and cucumber sandwiches, or the vegetarian wraps, or the lemon squares, or anything. It's all delicious and homemade. Open only for lunch, Monday through Friday; credit cards accepted only for orders of $25 or more. Call (803) 790–0733.

If you want to do Five Points right, you must eat at *Andy's Deli,* 2005 Greene Street. Andy Shlon has run his family business (along with his two very handsome sons) since 1978 and he's never met a stranger. "Hello, my dear" and "Hello, my friend" are mainstays, as are the big, thick, unbeatable sandwiches and salads. (Andy's Special and the R2D2 are good enough to keep bringing you back and back.) We defy you to find any better place in this state. Even if you did find deli food to match, you'd not find it in combination with such a friendly atmosphere. Cash and checks only, but Andy's been known to tell regulars to bring the money back another time if they forget and flip out a credit card with no George Washingtons to be found. If you're looking to be a regular, this place is for you. We just like to call it home. Open from 10:00 a.m. to 9:00 p.m., Monday through Saturday; closed Sunday. Call (803) 799–ANDY.

Al-Amir is the perfect restaurant if you are in the mood for some thoroughly scrumptious Middle Eastern fare that will fill up your stomach and leave your wallet full. The most expensive meal served is the baked kibbeh (an oven-baked blend of cracked wheat and ground beef, spices, and pine nuts served with a side of plain yogurt) for just under $10. Grape leaves, hummus, baba ghannouj (roasted eggplant blended with tahini), and kibbeh can be found in the appetizers or in the Al-Amir Sampler, and these are so good you might just want to order everything two or three times and forget about an entrée. Of course, it would be hard to turn down an entree such as a kabob, a shawarma, a tawouk, or a mudardara. If you don't know what these are, run, don't walk (no, drive!) as fast as you can and try them out. They're better tasted than described. Don't forget to top whatever it is you do eat with one of the fabulous under-$2.00 Al-Amir desserts. (We also highly recommend the yogurt salad.) This is Middle Eastern food done just right! Al-Amir is at 2930 Devine Street (803–771–6292).

Nestled directly behind the Adam's Mark Hotel in the heart of the heart of Columbia, at 1230 Hampton Street, where it has been for ten years, is Columbia's premier lunchtime spot: *The Hampton Place Cafe.* Not fancy but great! Specializing in gourmet sandwiches, homemade crab and spinach-mushroom quiches, and Greek and Caesar salads, owner Steve Gendel packs them in every day for lunch. The average price with drink is around $6.00. His only advice is that you get there early to get a seat. Open Monday through Friday 11:00 a.m. to 3:00 p.m. Call (803) 254–5847. Check it out at www.jobscolumbiasc.com/hampton.

Hampton Place is a great spot to use as a center for seeing the new downtown Columbia. One block away is the wonderfully set up *Columbia Museum of Art,* Main and Hampton Streets (803–799–2810), which houses a truly fabulous permanent collection. See page 000 or visit www.colmusart.org.

Across the street from the museum is *Rising High,* 1508 Main Street (803–252–6111), which has three locations in Columbia. This is a marvelous renovation of the Art Deco Kress Dime Store Building from the 1930s. Almost all the artifacts and decorations have been preserved, as well as the entire front facade, which is covered with gold leaf. It's a masterpiece of renovation and a brilliant landmark in Columbia's new downtown recovery. From Rising High, you can stroll three blocks down Main to the State House and the surrounding parks.

About a mile south of the capitol, the *Rosewood Market and Deli,* at 2803 Rosewood Drive, is a one-of-a-kind success story for natural and organic foods. The deli operates six days a week and features hot meals twice daily. Much of the food here has a macrobiotic slant, but some dairy and fish are occasionally used. Cooking classes are held in the kitchen here on Sundays. On any given day you can find local and international artists happily spooning up their tofu on the outside patio. Call (803) 765–1083 or visit www.rosewoodmarket.com.

The only quotable line from Immanuel Kant runs, "David Hume shook me from my dogmatic slumbers." Which brings me to Tom Elliott, the ex-treasurer and representative for Richland County. Tom, who was deep into retirement, was shaken from his slumbers by golf. Not only did he take it up and buy a set of sticks and begin playing every day, he wound up owning the *Columbia East Driving Range* so he could practice. The range is 3 miles past the Veteran's Hospital on Garner's Gerry Road and is directly across from an open-air produce market, which sells everything from watermelons and okra to hot, boiled peanuts.

Tom, when he's not playing golf, presides over the counter here and over the years has attracted a group of regulars who look and act not unlike the cast of *Cheers* but with more political savvy and much better material.

But it's not all fun and games out at Columbia East. Tom does a lively business on the driving range, which is lighted for as far as the eye can see and stays open until the last person stops swinging. Inside, he has an array of new and used clubs, and if you like he can assemble almost anything you want including stock heads, shafts, and grips. He also has golf caps, bags, gloves, and umbrellas. In short, if you play the game, this is where you can get everything at an affordable price. As for balls, this is the place to go to save some serious money. Slightly used Titleists, which normally cross the counter when new at $3.00 a pop, are only two for a dollar, and you won't be able to find a blemish or a scratch. Sound advice: Load up on these as well as Maxflis, Wilsons, etc.

Tom also sells Vienna sausage, pickled eggs, hot dogs, fruit cakes, dill pickles, beer, soft drinks, and small-bore candies and mints. You'll find Tom at 8041 Garner's Ferry Road. Call (803) 695–1220.

Minglewood Music at 800 Harden Street (803–254–9999) is a great place to keep in mind for almost any kind of fast food served at almost any hour. The restaurant also has a pool table, video games, a comfortable bar, outdoor seating right in the heart of Five Points, and a lively crowd of steady customers. You can sit outside, eat, listen to the juke box music, and watch the 20-odd-foot fountain lighting up the night. Hours are Monday through Wednesday 8:00 to 2:00 a.m. and Thursday through Saturday 8:00 to 4:00 a.m.

If you're really hungry, visit *Gilligan's Barbecue and Seafood* at 2006 Senate Street, which is perhaps my favorite spot for sheer color, food, and activity. Behind the ragtag bar is an autographed eight-by-ten of Bob Denver from *Gilligan's Island*—he's visited here once and approved of everything Tim Petersen, the owner, has done to duplicate the old sitcom feeling. The building, which looks as if it's been slung together with driftwood and sheet iron signs, fits snugly up under a truly wonderful magnolia tree, and flowing out in all directions we find the following: a full-scale sand volleyball court, a croquet court, a bocce court, a Ping-Pong table, horseshoes, and enough room out on the grass for outdoor dining for a couple hundred. Inside there are darts, a full-sized pool table, and enough memorabilia to keep anyone gawking.

Tim also prides himself on his seafood dishes and his barbecue, all at reasonable prices ranging from $6.00 to $9.00. And if you would like a sermon on barbecue, this is the spot to stop because Tim is the man to listen to. He prides himself on serving only barbecue from what in the trade is called "three rib down," which translates into only small, expensive hogs of less than 110 pounds, which in turn means less fat. He actually closes his eyes and shudders when he mentions barbecue buffets where you can eat all you want. "Man, all that fat will kill you quicker than a train." He says the longer, bigger ribs served in those places are from hogs weighing considerably more than 110, more like 400 and up, with two and three times the amount of fat. But there's more to barbecue than just high-low fat percentages. What you'll want to do is have a beer here with him and find out about barbecue sauces and seafood and how

South Carolina State Fair—Late October

Part of the joy of living down here in the "hard lard belt" and celebrating surviving the summers is fall and the **South Carolina State Fair** in late October. It's the biggest extravaganza down here. There is nothing even close to it. For exact days, call (803) 256–2941, or visit www.scstatefair.org. A few of the contests are biscuit making from scratch, Rebel yells, clogging, chicken impersonations, hog steeplechases, and duck slides. And through it all are more lights, neon, and calliope and country music than the average person can stand. One wag calls the country music "ignorance set to music." If you decide to go, take my advice, lose a few pounds before you set foot on the premises because every red-blooded church in town has a food booth and everything is knock-down delicious.

Last year, for no apparent reason, I drifted over to the Hog Show and asked a few questions that I'd been saving up for a few years. The big one was how the judges pick a champion hog. The judge I cornered told me more than I wanted to know; this man had all the facts. "Friend, we judge hogs on one point and one point only: how much meat that fellow can deliver. If there's one extra pork chop on that hog, I don't care if he's got one eye and four ears, that hog is our number one. Friend, raising hogs is a business, this ain't no kennel club." He kept calling me friend. "Friend, you got to figure the less overall fat, the more hog you'll get for your money. Now take a fat, wide fellow with a lot of extra jowl hanging down. That hog ain't good for nothing. And I mean nothing, in my estimation, turns a judge off faster than a hog that can't walk."

I asked him why, if everything was so slide-ruled out for the butcher counter, the owners hot-combed and powdered the hogs before showing. "Well friend, it's the exact same reason a girl will primp in front of a mirror. Showmanship! They want that hog to step out there with the best possible chance." He handed me a tract and a bumper sticker, HOGS ARE BEAUTIFUL. "We're out to improve the image of the hog and maybe bring a little of that beef money down to us. Lot of people figure hogs are dirty and will eat anything you put in front of them. Friend, you give a hog a chance and he'll live a lot cleaner than most people." So much for hogs.

he makes his delicious coleslaw and hush puppies. A place you'll not want to miss. Needless to say, dress is casual. Call (803) 252–5252.

One of the most enjoyable things I did while researching this book was walk in the **Francis Beidler Forest** at Four Holes Swamp in Harleyville. To get there from Columbia, take I–26 south to exit 187 and follow the signs to the forest. A 1½-mile boardwalk takes you through the largest remaining virgin stand of bald cypress and tupelo gum trees in the world. It is truly awesome. Many of these forest giants rising out of the clear pools and blackwater streams are 1,000 years old, or older, and reach up well over 200 feet. Alligators, snakes, and every conceivable native animal can be seen if you are quiet and stand still. In the evenings you can even see owls and an occasional otter. A self-guiding tour booklet leads you through this natural cathedral in the forest. It's a walk you will never, ever forget.

The forest is named for the lumberman-conservationist Francis Beidler, who preserved the area from logging. Unconventional for a lumberman of his time, he allowed much of his timber to stand while taxes, interest, hurricanes, and insects took their toll. After his death in 1924, his family and later the National Audubon Society and the Nature Conservancy raised the money to continue his program and even expand the sanctuary. Today it covers almost 6,000 spectacular acres. If I had one place to visit in South Carolina and only one, I'd go here. Open to the public from 9:00 a.m. to 5:00 p.m. Tuesday through Sunday. Closed Monday, Thanksgiving, December 24, 25, and 31, and January 1. Admission for adults is $7.00; children six to eighteen pay $3.50; children under six are admitted free, as are Audubon Life Members. Call (803) 462–2150 or write Sanctuary Manager, Francis Beidler Forest, 336 Sanctuary Road, Harleyville 29448. Their Web site is www.audubon.org/local/sanctuary/beidler.

And finally, the absolute most enjoyable thing I did while working on this book was having Tuesday night breakfast served from midnight to 3:00 a.m. at *The Capitol Restaurant,* 1210 Main Street (803–765–0176), in the winter when the legislature was in session. If you start with your back facing the statue of the Confederate soldier in front of the steps of the capitol and walk up Main Street for half a block, you'll see the old and fading green awning of the Capitol Restaurant. It's usually open for breakfast and lunch from 7:00 a.m. to 3:00 p.m. Monday through Saturday, closed Sunday. The Capitol features breakfasts of sausage, eggs, and grits served all day long; you can also get steaks and chops. Everything is good and everything is served speedily and is modestly priced. A steak with all the trimmings crosses the finish line at about $9.00.

The Capitol Restaurant

If there is such a place as the exact center of Columbia, and maybe even all of South Carolina, where the wires, the politics, and the liaisons all come together, the Capitol Restaurant is it, and it's been this way for the past fifty or so years. It all happens on Tuesday night while the legislature is in session—from the second Tuesday in January to the end of the first week in June. The house band on these Tuesdays includes Commissioner Rudolph Mitchell on keyboard, Commissioner Cecil Bowers on fiddle, and commission employees Oscar Coates and Roy Gainey playing guitars and harmonizing on the songs. The music ranges far and wide from Jimmy Rodgers's blue yodels to Merle Haggard, from Baptist hymns to "Danny Boy" and anything country-modern that's in the air. Local and not-so-local talent show up and take the mike, and once in a while they'll even sing their favorite song. Kurt Vonnegut once croaked out "Red River Valley," and over the years John Irving, Tom Wolfe, Pat Conroy, Garrison Keillor, James Dickey, Nora Ephron, Pauline Kael, Stephen Spender, John Gardner, and Bruce Springsteen have all taken the mike and said, "Hello, I'm sure glad to be here."

The high point of the Tuesday nights here is the wild and woolly rendition of "Orange Blossom Special," with Cecil smoking on his fiddle and congressmen and the local citizens heel-and-toe clogging in the aisles, yipping out enough yeeeee-haaaaws to keep the beer glasses rattling. After the reverberations die down—it takes a while—a hush comes over the room as Oscar Coates chords his guitar and lets the sound hang in the air. Then he'll lean in on the microphone: "OK. Now remember. No dancing during gospel." And he'll segue into "I'll Fly Away," singing with an intensity of feeling that brings tears to the eyes of the faithful and is absolutely beyond description.

There will be a private party sign on the door; ignore it and come on in and ask for John. Or hell, ask for me. Hours are Monday through Saturday 7:00 a.m. to 3:00 p.m., Sunday 8:00 a.m. to 3:00 p.m.

While doing this book, I've used the word best only a couple of times. Well, here's one more, but this one would be a mortal sin to leave out—the best breads and muffins in all of South Carolina. *Rising High* at 827 Harden Street in Five Points, a hundred yards from the fountain, has its own bakery and specializes in using only fresh and natural ingredients. My advice is to come before 11:30 a.m. or after 2:00 p.m. because the lunch rushes here are fierce. My favorite muffin here is the cranberry, where there is just enough muffin to hold the cranberries together. Owned and operated by two enterprising locals, Kirkman Finlay and Brian Owen, this is an ideal spot to stop for breakfast or lunch or to pick up a loaf of bread or a great box lunch for the road. Call (803) 254-3113. The Web site is www.risinghighcafe.com.

If you are in Columbia on a Saturday night, a spot you shouldn't miss is ***Bill's Music Shop and Pickin Parlor*** at 710 Meeting Street (803–796–6477). Some of the best bluegrass groups in the country play here and, after they decide they like it, sometimes stay for four and five weeks. Admission is $10 at the door, and it's worth every penny. Once in a while, for special occasions, the admission is a covered dish. If you decide to bring one, don't show up with any alcohol. Check out www.billsmusicshop.com.

Jim Casey's Discount Fireworks Emporium at 3830 Rosewood is probably the wildest mix of products and entertainment you'll see on the East Coast. First of all, they're the biggest seller of fireworks in the state. Second, they have a New Orleans–type restaurant—they grind their own coffee beans. Third, they have an all-night night club and cabaret, which features great bands and great entertainment, Karaoke, and a bar that seems to never close.

If you're lucky enough to see Jack Casey or his son John, they'll give you an education about the fireworks industry. Basically the Japanese, who have had some recovery in their economy during the past fifty years, have stopped making fireworks. The reason is there were too many explosions and too many casualties. An example Jack cites is Roman candles. He says in order to produce a good Roman candle you have to pack the powder down as tight as possible. But the catch is, if you pack it too tight, it blows up. Nowadays most of the Roman candles are produced in China.

Another trend in fireworks is the drop in popularity in the old macho exploders, i.e., torpedoes, cherry bombs, 6-inch-long firecrackers, etc. Today the women, who are doing most of the buying, are insisting on more safety and more colors. The big sellers are now sparklers, fountains, sprays, and much more colorful exploding rockets. A few of the newer Chinese products are Celestial Spider, Mammoth Chrysanthemum, Golden Spider, Crackling Delight, Blinking Dragon's Breath, and Fountain with Thunderclaps. Casey's phone is (803) 738–9173.

At 116 State Street you can find a row of restaurants, including the very quaint and very cool ***House Coffee.*** It has outdoor seating and the atmosphere is straight comfort. On any given day you will find high school students mixed with college students mixed with business executives, all talking to each other and enjoying the wide range of espressos and delicious food.

While you're there, you may want to have one of their "House Specials," which would consist of any number of different sandwiches and include pasta and a very fresh fruit salad (a real seller!). They also have a most unique espresso menu, with the leading sellers being the Almond JayED: Is this correct? or is it an Almond Joy? (a mochaccino steamed with almond syrup and topped with whipped cream) and the Milky Way (a mochaccino steamed with caramel syrup and topped with whipped cream). On a hot day, be sure to ask for an Iced Milky Way!

Food is served until midnight, and get this, the most you'll pay for a regular meal with tea is $5.75. Not bad! And if you're lucky enough to get there on Thursday nights, you'll hear live acoustic music (and you might even catch some classical tunes from Columbia star, Ray Thom!). Hours are 11:30 a.m. to midnight Monday through Saturday and noon to midnight on Sunday. Call (803) 791–5663.

On the same street, at 100 State Street, is **Mangia Mangia,** a very upscale, uptown Italian restaurant. Reservations are required, and they have valet parking! The menu is quite extensive and will run you anywhere from $7.00 to $8.00—if you order one of the delicious and filling appetizers—to around $22.00 for an entree with wine. You won't want to miss their osso bucco, a traditional Italian dish made up of a roasted lamb shank, Tuscan beans, potatoes, carrots, and onions. You'll feel as if you are in another city eating here; it is dark and romantic, yet cosmopolitan and usually very crowded, and always fun. This is an exciting restaurant owned by Paul Chernoff, and often you will find his sister, Jessie, handing out menus and a million-buck smile! Open Monday through Thursday 5:00 to 10:00 p.m. and Friday and Saturday from 5:00 to 11:00 p.m. (However, the fabulous bar is open until the last customer leaves—always a good sign!) Closed on Sunday. Call (803) 791–3443. Their Web site is www.mangiamangiasc.com.

Fifteen or so miles out Route 75, almost to Sumter, is the sprawling **Mr. Bunky's General Store** at 10441 Garner's Ferry Road, Hopkins (803–783–3501). As they say in the trades, "Here you will find anything." For once it's true. Name it and it's here. From horse saddles to crickets and worms to fresh baked goods. From cook stoves, shovels, and rakes to boiled peanuts, fresh meat, and produce: local watermelons, grapes, strawberries, peaches, and cantaloupes. On one wing is a full-sized buffet restaurant that serves three meals a day, and on the second floor out behind the homemade rocking chairs and bird houses sits a white cockatoo called "Mr. Sunshine." The kids love him and crowd around while he preens and tells them what's going on in the bird world. If you like fishing and forgot your tackle, you can get everything you can possibly need for fly casting, bait casting, pole fishing, or even frog gigging. Mr. Bunky, or one of his relatives, will be glad to give you all the information about where to go and what to use for bait.

One more barbecue stop, but this one is different. It's open Tuesday through Saturday from 11:00 a.m. to 9:00 p.m. Owned and operated by Gerald and Carolyn Meyer, with Carolyn's sister Diane helping out, **Meyer's Barbecue House** in Blythewood is one of the fastest-growing restaurants in this part of the state. The place is small and if you miss the Blythewood cutoff, 18 miles north of Columbia on I–77, it's very hard to find. If you do miss it, ask anyone you see. Everyone knows about it. On the other hand, if you make the cutoff when you're supposed to and go 500 yards to the right, there it is on the right.

Once inside this clean, well-lighted but small establishment, you have a choice of barbecued pork or chicken with sides of potato salad, corn, yams, slaw, green beans, and baked beans. And that is it. But that is enough. In the event you can't decide what barbecue and what sauce you want, they will serve you a free sample. Everything here is first rate, cooked on the premises, and the prices are easygoing. A barbecue sandwich is $3.25; chicken, $3.00. Sides are extra but with a soft drink and a side, you can get out of there for less than $6.00. If you decide to eat here, which I did, extra sauce of your choice is served in a squeeze bottle. Excellent for take-out and large catered affairs. Call (803) 754–7400.

To reach **Lexington Arms** from downtown Columbia take Highway 1, 14 miles north to 314 West Main Street, Lexington. Around here Highway 1 is called the Two Notch Road, until it gets out of town. Then it changes to U.S. Highway 1 and goes on about its business as it runs on up the road to Maine. It begins at the first phone pole in Florida down at Key West. Anyway, this is the home of Elizabeth and Duncan Crowe and their five children and probably the best and most varied menu in the Carolinas and Georgia.

At fifteen, in the famous Swiss hotel school, La Ron, Elizabeth was one of the few women enrolled, but while the others wanted to be dietitians, she began her career as a chef. Today, she says, despite the hard work and long

Lexington Arms

hours, some of her happiest moments were at La Ron, where she learned the fine art of German and French cuisine. "I still remember those chefs dressed in white with their silver spoons around their necks." When she finished school, she had planned to return to her home in Heidelburg to help her mother open a cafe, but being independent, she followed a different course. "I ran away. My mother always had big plans of opening a hotel and dining club. She was going to be the boss and I was going to do all the work. In Europe, women in the kitchen were usually paid lower wages and often forced to give away their cooking secrets. With my papers from La Ron, I knew I could always get work in America, or, for that matter, anywhere."

Elizabeth's husband, Duncan, whom she met in Kansas City, where she was manager of the Riverboat Restaurant, was born in London and began his career in the wine trade, working as a wine salesman. He went to the West Indies in the hotel business then transferred to Kansas City, where he met Elizabeth. After their marriage, they operated a resort hotel in Antigua and lived and worked in Florida before coming to Lexington and purchasing the Lexington Arms.

Elizabeth says she and Duncan have "some sort of aversion to big cities that developed when we lived on the island. It was small. Everybody knew everybody. That's why we are so happy here in Lexington." Duncan added that they wanted to establish the same kind of familiar atmosphere at the Lexington Arms. "We want it to develop into a community area, a cafe setting. We want people to feel it's their restaurant, whether they want a full meal or just a cup of coffee or a glass of beer. As a matter of fact, if you sit at the bar and decide to have a full meal there, that's fine with us."

From the outside, the Lexington Arms looks like a British pub. But Elizabeth and Duncan have taken great care to brighten up the interior and have made it casual and comfortable and a great place just to come in for a beer. The combination of Elizabeth's German, French, and Swiss cuisine and Duncan's British background has resulted in exactly what they wanted—a first-class restaurant that specializes in German, French, and Swiss cuisine, with, of course, many standard American entrees and Caribbean dishes, as well as a very fine and complete wine list.

The wine bar allows you to order some of the finest wines by the glass—the perfect way to try something new. Elizabeth and Duncan's sons, Charles and Phillip, both now chefs, help out in the kitchen, so the Crowe dynasty is in very good shape for many, many years to come. Hours are 5:30 p.m. to midnight Monday through Saturday. Closed Sunday. German dishes are served only on Monday, Thursday, and Saturday, and French dishes only on Tuesday and Wednesday. The lounge opens at 4:00 p.m. Call (803) 359–2700.

Richard Riley, former governor of South Carolina and Secretary of Education, once waved his arms and pronounced that Rhoten's sausage featured at **Rhoten's General Store** at 720 Main Street was the best of the best in the Palmetto State. Since that time there have been a few small changes: First, Rhoten's General Store went out of business; second, it is now in the mattress business. Today the old store is stacked to the ceiling and window levels with full-, queen-, and king-size mattresses. But the old ways die hard around here, and the populace insisted that they continue selling pork sausage, which they are doing. The result is the only store in the Western world that sells mattresses and pork sausage, and only mattresses and pork sausage. Former Secretary of Education Riley never endorsed the mattresses, but the folks around here feel sure he would if asked. They all say the mattresses are good, not quite as good as the sausage, but pretty close. So when you come through Lexington, come on in. There's a good chance you won't be in the market for a mattress, but if you get here in the cool months, you can load up on pork sausage. Hours at Rhoten's are 8:00 a.m. to 5:00 p.m. Monday through Saturday. Call (803) 359–6219.

Inside the **Flight Deck Restaurant** in downtown Lexington at 109A Old Chapin Road, there is something you simply cannot leave South Carolina without seeing—a 15-foot plastic cast of mighty King Kong straddling the Empire State Building. With his right hand he is holding on to the antenna on top of the building and glowering at the attacking planes that will eventually be his undoing, while with his left he is crushing a 6-foot model of a Stearman biplane. Your kids will be talking about this forever. Meanwhile, if there is any red blood in your system, you will be absolutely awestruck by the collection of incredible model planes that cover the ceiling, the foyers, and every inch of wall space. Now I'm not talking about hand-held models you wind up with rubber bands and fly across a room or down a hallway. I'm talking about a P-47 Thunderbolt with a 12-foot wingspan, an enormous P-51, huge B-17s, 24s, 29s, and modern jet fighters. The range is incredible and only a madman or someone like Ted Stambolitis, who owns and operates the place, would have dared do all this by himself. Yes, he built the planes, hung them, and knows every inch of each of them. And he will be delighted to show you around and answer any and all questions. Incidentally, Ted, also a licensed pilot, has actually flown everything from hang gliders to experimental aircraft.

But more than just a museum of old planes, the Flight Deck is a busy, very successful restaurant specializing in sandwiches, buffet meals, and desserts, including old-fashioned milkshakes and malteds made and served in old-time shake cans if you like them that way. Everything here is first rate, moderately priced, and exceptionally clean. It's an ideal place to bring, and maybe even leave, the kids. Hours are Monday through Thursday 11:00 a.m. to 9:30 p.m.,

Flight Deck Restaurant

Friday and Saturday 11:00 a.m. to 11:00 p.m. Closed Sunday. Call (803) 957–5990. You can see more of the ambiance at www.flightdeskrestaurant.net.

OK, a little stroll down memory lane. On the corner of Huger and Gervais right across from the new Publix Superstore is a wrought iron window. Back in the 1940s and 1950s my grandmother Fanny—Dad's mother—did a lively business in this tiny spot selling fish sandwiches and fish sandwiches only. First she would buy the fish from the folks fishing the river two blocks away. Then she would clean them and fry them in 450-degree lard and serve them between two slices of bread in a wax wrapper with a pickle chip on top for a dime. The customers would bring their own soft drinks and sit on the Gervais Street curb watching the Fords and Chevys go by, or on the Huger Street side looking down at the river two blocks away. The fish sandwich was served with the head and tail intact and most of the customers ate everything except the long spinal column. Now you talk about fine dining. Anyhow, Grandma did a lively business right here.

And why am I telling you all this? It's because right here in the heart of the heart of the capital city at 1124 Taylor Street is the ***Silver Moon Restaurant,*** (803) 799–1855, where they serve a fish sandwich that brings tears to my eyes when I crunch down on that dorsal fin and remember every millimeter of Grandma's Fish House.

The Silver Moon also serves breakfast, hamburgers, and a fried pork chop sandwich with the bone in it that is a true wonder. The fresh fish is whiting and comes with the head off. Stop by and save some money and eat something you'll never forget. The Silver Moon also serves breakfast, lunch, and dinner. There's no wine list here but everything is first rate. I'll take a polygraph on this one. That's, as they say, a wrap.

Places to Stay in Uplands and Columbia

COLUMBIA

Chestnut Cottage B&B
1718 Hampton Street
(803) 256–1718
www.chestnutcottage.com

Rose Hall B&B
1006 Barnwell Street
(803) 771–2288
www.rosehallbb.com

EDGEFIELD

Cedar Grove Plantation
1365 Highway 25 North
(803) 637–3056

GREENVILLE

Creekside Plantation
3118 South Highway 14
(864) 297–3293

Pettigru Place B&B
302 Pettigru Street
(864) 242–4529
www.pettigruplace.com

LANDRUM

Country Mouse Inn
120 North Trade Avenue
(864) 457–4061

Red Horse Inn
310 North Campbell Road
(864) 895–4968
www.theredhorseinn.com

ROCK HILL

Book & Spindle
626 Oakland Avenue
(803) 328–1913

East Main Guest House
600 East Main
(803) 366–1161

SALEM

Sunrise Farm B&B
325 Sunrise Drive
(864) 944–0121

SPARTANBURG

Nicholls-Crook Plantation B&B
120 Plantation Drive,
Woodruff
(864) 476–8820

Walnut Lane B&B
110 Ridge Road, Lyman
(864) 949–7230
www.walnutlaneinn.com

UNION

Inn at Merridun
100 Merridun Place
(864) 427–7052
www.merridun.com

Juxa Plantation
117 Wilson Road
(864) 427–8688

Places to Eat in Uplands and Columbia

BUFFALO

Midway Barbecue
811 Hash Boulevard
(869) 427–4047

COLUMBIA

Dianne's on Devine
2400 Devine Street
(803) 254–3535
www.diannesondevine.com

Garibaldi's
2013 Greene Street
(803) 771–8888

Goatfeathers Coffee Bar & Restaurant
2017 Devine Street
(803)256–3325

Longhorn Steakhouse
902 Gervais Street, Suite A
(803) 254–5100

Motor Supply Company
920 Gervais Street
(803) 256–6687
www.motorsupplycobistro
.com

Za's Brick Oven Pizza
2930 Devine Street
(803) 771–7334

GREENVILLE

Cafe & Then Some
101 College Street
(864) 232–2287
www.cafeats.com

SPARTANBURG

Gerhard's Cafe
1200 East Main Street,
West Columbia
(864) 591–1920

Mangia Mangia
100 State Street
(803) 791–3443
www.mangiamangiasc.com

Indexes

Entries for museums and plantations appear in the special indexes on page 152.

Village Bed and Breakfast, The, 52
Vulcan Rock Quarry, 130

War Memorial Building, 39
Ward's Barbeque, 88
Westin Poinsett Hotel, 101
White Point Garden, 3, 20
Whitmarsh, 35
Wild Dunes, 25
Wildwater, Ltd., 114
Willcox Inn, 91
Winnsboro, 82
Winthrop University, 115
Winyah Bay, 58, 62
Wofford College, 112
Woodrow Wilson's Boyhood
    Home, 123

Yawkey, Tom, 62
Yawkey Wildlife Center, 62
Yesterday's Restaurant and
    Tavern, 127
Yorktown, 18

Za's, 132

Museums
Aiken County Historical Museum, 91
Andrews Old Town Hall
    Museum, 59

Beaufort Museum, 37
Charleston Museum, The, 22
Columbia Museum of Art, 117, 135
Edisto Museum, The, 30
Florence Museum of Art, Science,
    and History, 80
Gibbes Museum of Art, 10
Greenville Museum of Art, 101
Museum of Coastal Carolina, 74
Museum of York County, 114
Original Benjamin's Calabash
    Seafood and Nautical Museum,
    The, 73
Patriot's Point Naval and Maritime
    Museum, 18
Rice Museum, 57
Shoeless Joe Jackson Museum, 103
South Carolina Railroad Museum, 83
South Carolina State Museum, 118

Plantations
Boone Hall, 17
Grimball Plantation, 29
Hampton Plantation, The, 54
Lowndes Grove Plantation, 3
Middleton Place, 13
Shipyard Plantation, 47

About the Authors

William Price Fox grew up in the Low Country of South Carolina. He has worked as a salesman in New York, a scriptwriter in Hollywood, and a professor at the Writer's Workshop at the University of Iowa. He is the author of seven novels and short story collections, including *Southern Fried Plus Six, Ruby Red, Chitlin Strut & Other Madrigals,* and *Wild Blue Yonder.* His latest book is *Satchel Paige's America,* from the University of Alabama Press. His articles and short stories have been published in magazines and newspapers such as *Sports Illustrated, Travel & Leisure, Golf Digest, Esquire, The Saturday Evening Post,* and the *Los Angeles Times.* A movie has been made based on his stories, *108 Stitches.* He currently is the producer and moderator of the University of South Carolina E.T.V. Writer's Workshop Program and lives in Columbia.

J. Michael McLaughlin has been living in and writing about the Low Country since 1979. His writing has found its way into numerous regional and national magazines, and his freelance work as an advertising and public relations consultant has captured national marketing awards. Michael graduated from Indiana University in 1967 with a B.S. degree in business-journalism, aiming for a Madison Avenue career in advertising. Instead, his first writing job turned out to be in Vietnam, where, as a war correspondent, he won a Bronze Star for his coverage of the 101st Airborne Division during the ill-fated 1968 Tet Offensive. Michael has also co-authored *Insiders' Guide to Charleston* and *It Happened in South Carolina,* both for The Globe Pequot Press.